ACCOMACK TITHABLES

1663–1695

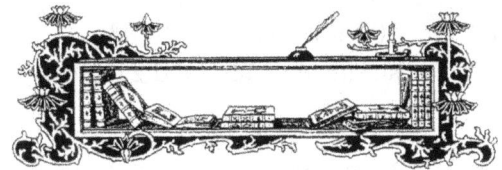

Compiled by

Stratton Nottingham

HERITAGE BOOKS
2009

HERITAGE BOOKS
AN IMPRINT OF HERITAGE BOOKS, INC.

Books, CDs, and more—Worldwide

For our listing of thousands of titles see our website
at
www.HeritageBooks.com

Published 2009 by
HERITAGE BOOKS, INC.
Publishing Division
100 Railroad Ave. #104
Westminster, Maryland 21157

Copyright © 1931 Stratton Nottingham

Other Heritage Books by Stratton Nottingham:
Accomack (Virginia) Land Causes, 1728-1825
Accomack County, Virginia Certificates and Rights, 1663-1709; and Tithables, 1663-1695
Accomack Tithables, 1663-1695
Marriage License Bonds of Northumberland County, Virginia: from 1783 to 1850
Revolutionary Soldiers and Sailors from Lancaster County, Virginia
Soldiers and Sailors of the Eastern Shore of Virginia in the Revolutionary War
Virginia Land Causes: Lancaster County, 1795-1848; Northampton County, 1731-1868
Wills and Administrations of Accomack, 1663-1800

All rights reserved. No part of this book may be reproduced or transmitted in any form or by any means, electronic or mechanical, including photocopying, recording or by any information storage and retrieval system without written permission from the author, except for the inclusion of brief quotations in a review.

International Standard Book Numbers
Paperbound: 978-1-58549-262-6
Clothbound: 978-0-7884-8290-8

FOREWORD

One of the most valuable sources of information relative to the early generations of Virginia families are the lists of tithables, or tax lists. These lists enable the researcher to establish the locality in which many of our early ancestors first settled, and, when the tithables are recorded in other counties, to follow them with more or less accuracy when they moved on. Unfortunately all of the counties did not record these lists, but those of Northampton and Accomack were, and have, among other things, proved invaluable in connecting many of the families of these two counties with Sussex, Delaware, and Somerset, Worcester and other counties of Lower Maryland.

The lists in this volume have been carefully copied and verified by the compiler, and it is his sincere hope that it will prove to be of value to those interested in the history and genealogy of Virginia.

ACCOMACK TITHABLES (Tax Lists): 1663 - 1695

A List of Tithables in Accomack County A. D. 1663

Name	Tithes	Name	Tithes	Name	Tithes
Mr Anto. Hodgkins	4	Mrs. Charlton	1	Alex: Adison	3
John Ramy	6	Tobius Sellvey	1	Edw: More	2
George Truett	5	Robt. Bayly	2	Charles Ratclife	5
Jno. Williams	4	Richard Johnson	1	Geo: Johnson	4
Jno. Jenkins	3	Anto. Johnson	2	Wm. Rodolphus	2
Tho: Leatherbury	1	Michill Ricords	4	James Price	4
Edward Revell	3	Mr. Jno. Wise	7	Wm. Taylor	4
Wm. Silverthorne	2	Jno. Alford	3	Hen: Bishop	5
Anto. Longo	1	Mr. Southee Littleton	5	Edw: Smith	2
Robert Hill	4			Geo: Crump	2
Dermon Shellowan	2	Teage Andrews	5	Tho: Tunnell	2
Jno. Lewis	5	John Watts	2	Jno. Macele	2
Jno. Turnor	2	Thomas Benthall	5	Tho: Newton	2
Rich: Kellum	7	Wm. Chase	6	Jno. Holding	2
Jno. Fawsett	2	Wm. & Francis		Mr. Geo: Hack	9
Jno. Walthom	6	Benstone	3	John Parker	6
Rich: Buckland	1	Alphanso Ball	3	Richard Hill	6
Cristop: Calvert	3	Jno. Cobb	1	John Die	1
Capt. Geo: Parker	8	James Camell	1	John Lewis	5
Jno. Brookes	1	Nath: Bradford	4	Walter Taylor	5
Hendrick Johnson	1	Samuell Taylor	2	Hone Collony	2
Old Richard at Mr.		Robt: Richinson	3	Wm. Alworth	1
Wheelers		Mr. Tho: Fookes	10	Mr. Edm: Bowman	9
Abraham Taylor	1	Mr. Hugh Yeo	7	Wm. Major	3
John Eyres	3	Daniell Ograhan	1	Obedience Johnson	3
Robt. Hewitt	6	Hen: Edwards	4	Wm. White	1
John Cross	1	Jno. Waler	3	Daniell Macra	1
Simon Miller	1	Andrew Finee	4	Jno. Milby	3
Rich: Hill	1	Mrs. Jordan	8	Jno. Major	3
Bartholomew Man	1	Tho. Bloyes	2	Jno. Durmon	3
Jeames Atkinson	1	Jonas Jackson	2	Robt. Brace	3
John Smith	4	Richard Stevens	4	Mr. Jno. West	7
Arthur Upshott	3	Tho: Davis	1	Mr. Devorx. Browne	12
Henry Smith	6	Jno. Paramore	3	Folcat Obin	2
Tho: Selve	1	Ralph Dow	2	Jno. King	1
Robt. Hicknet	2	Phillip Fisher	4	Jno. Haggaman	1
Jno. Johnson	2	Tho: Carrell	2	Edm: Kelly	4
Majr. Jno. Tilney	8	Timothy Coe	4	Wm. Smith	2
Henry Stott	2	Richard Smith	2	Mr. Leving Denwood	5
Tho: Browne	3	Wm. Roberts	5	Henry Browne	2
Wm. Blake	2	Benjamen Larance	1	Robt. Watson	1
Henry White	1	Tho: Wally	2	Jno. Prittyman	2
Tho: Smith	1	Geo: Brickhouse	2	Jno. Stutson	4
Jeffry Minshall	3	Tho: Bell	1		

Sum Totall 409 - v. i - p. 35

List of Tithables in Accomack County A. Dom. 1664

Name	Tithes	Name	Tithes	Name	Tithes
Mr. Jno. Wise	5	Rich: Prichard	2	Michill Ricketts	4
Robt. Brase	3	Anto. Johnson	3	Tho: Newton	5

1

ACCOMACK TITHABLES (Tax Lists): 1663 - 1695

Name	Tithes	Name	Tithes	Name	Tithes
Capt. Geo: Parker	6	Tobias Selby	1	Jno. Lewis	8
John Barnet	1	Wm. Abram	1	Rich: Hill	6
Jno. Alford	4	Jno. Renny	6	Tho: Fowkes	4
James Atkins	1	Danll. Ograhan	1	Mr. Smith	4
Simon Millard	1	Jno. Watts, Coop.	1	George Crump	1
Geo: Trewett	3	David Williamson	1	Jno. Williams	4
Anto. Longo	1	Teage Andrews	2	Gausalin VanNitsinl	
Francis Sherwood	2	Tho: Tunell	3	Francis Benston	3
Mr. Southee Littleton	6	Mr. Jno. Parker	6	Mr. Geo: Hack	8
Mr. Jno. Wise	3	Wm. Chase	3	Tho: Leatherbury	4
John Brookes	1	Walter Taylor	4	Jno. Holden	2
Jno. Jenkins	1	Cristop: Calvert	2	Wm. Silverthorne	1
Wm. Darby	1	Robt: Hutchinson	4	Wm. Wilson	1
James Bonwell	4	Coll Edm: Scarburgh	27	John Watts	2
Mr. Devorx. Browne	15	John Die	1	Mrs. Charlton	1
James Fowkes	1	Owen Ocolnon	2	Mr. Hugh Yeo	8
Richard Kellum	7	Edw: Revell	4	Jno. Turnor	2
Mr. Anto. Hodgkins	4	Jno. Walthom	6	Susan Richardson	2
Jeffry Minshall	3	Wm. Rodolphus	2	Nath: Bradford	3
Obedience Johnson	2	Tho: Smith	1	Mr. Fawcett	5
Jno. Mekittick	3	Edw: Hammon	2	Jno. Wallop	2
David Wheatly	4	Robt. Huitt	8	William Smith	3
Alphanso Ball	2	Andrew Fenney	4	Jno. Drumon	3
Edward Moore	3	Mr. Bowman	11	Phillip Fisher	6
Wm. White	1	Giles Cope	4	Majr. Jno. Tilney	5
Jno. Studson	3	Henry Bishopp	5	Ralph Doe	2
Edw: Smith	3	Robt. Hignet	1	Jonah Jackson	3
George Brickhouse	2	Geo: Johnson	4	Jno. Hagaman	2
Henry Browne	1	Danll. Quillion	2	James Price	3
Mr. Denwood	6	Timothy Coe	5	Rich: Cox	1
Charles Rackliff	6	Samuell Jones	2	Henry Smith	5
Alexander Adison	5	Thomas Marshall	2	Jno. Prittyman	1
Henry Edwards	3	Rich: Smith	1	Edm: Kelly	4
Edw: Dolby	3	Jno. Smith	2	Wm. Blake	1
Jno. Sturgis	2	Wm. Roberts	6	Mrs. Jordan	6
Tho: Carrell	1	Thomas selby	1	Wm. Alworth	1
Thomas Browne	4	Wm. Taylor	4	Jno. Paramoore	3
Larence Teage	1	Henry White	2	Jno. Trotman	1
Wm. Jamor	3	Jno. Cutting	1	Danll Ecion	1
Jno. Goring	1	Thomas Bell	1	Fulcard Obin	3
Henry Stott	2	Robt. Watson	2		

Sum Totall 424 - v. i - p. 72

A List of Tithables in Accomack County A. D. 1665

Name	Tithes	Name	Tithes	Name	Tithes
Coll Edm: Scarburgh	33	Danll. Ograhan	1	Mr. Robt: Pitt	5
Wm. Darby	1	Jno. Anderson	3	James Bonwell	4
Mr. Jolly	6	Mr. Hugh Yeo	9	Geo: Johnson	4
Capt. Edm: Bowman	5	Mr. Anto. Hodgkins	5	Abram Taylor	2
Robt. Hutchinson	2	Jno. Eyre	4	Francis Sherwood	2
Richard Bayly	6	Mr. Tho: Fowke	5	Rich: Bundick	2
Robt. Huett	6	Jno. Jenkins	1	Wm. Dine	2

ACCOMACK TITHABLES (Tax Lists): 1663 - 1695

Name	Tithes	Name	Tithes	Name	Tithes
Geo: Truet	3	Wm. White	1	David Willisome	3
Tho: Hall	3	Francis Benston	2	Dermond Correne	1
Wm. Benston	1	Andrew Finne	2	Jno. Williams	5
Owen Collona	3	Jno. Watts, Coop:	2	Mr. Browne	15
Jno. Parker	5	Jno. Drumon	3	Tege Anderson	3
Wm. Ebourne	2	Edw: Revell	3	Jno. Barnet	1
Jno. Watts, taylor	3	Tobius Sellvey	4	Wm. Silverthorne	1
Robt: Brace	2	Jno. Renny	4	Richard Johnson	1
Alexandr. Massy	2	Michill Ricketts	4	Richard Hill	6
Thomas Tunnell	3	Jno. Wallop	2	Mr. Littleton	6
Wm. Custis	4	Jno. Mikeele	3	Tho: Leatherberry	6
Jno. Holding	1	James Fookes	4	Wm. Houton	1
Jno. Lewis	6	Richard Cox	1	Tho: Ryly &	
Mrs. Hack	6	Wm. Willson	1	Roger Turner	2
Xp: Calvert	2	Wm. Chase	4	Jno. Fawsett	6
Jno. Brookes	1	Joseph Harrison	1	Richard Buckland	1
Jno. Paramore	3	Anto. Longo	1	Geo: Hamling	2
Walter Taylor	7	Dermon Selevant	3	Mr. Jno. Wise	7
Edw: Hiching	1	Edw: Moore	4	Jno. Turnor	3
Hen: Bishopp	5	Jno. Willis	1	Edward Smith	3
Peter Sevorne	1	Thomas Marshall	2	Samll Showell	1
Jno. Smith	3	Barth: Meeres	1	James Comwell	1
Mary Paramore	3	Henry Browne	1	Henry Edwards	4
Thomas Selby	1	Mr. Jno. West	8	Wm. Alworth	1
Jno. Prittyman	1	Samuel Jones	2	Ralph Dow	2
Charles Rackleff	5	Hen: Stott	2	Jeffry Minshall	3
Thomas Allygood	1	Thomas Browne	3	Wm. Major	3
Henry White	2	Wm. Taylor	5	Edm: Kelly	4
Henry Smith	9	Tho: Carrell	1	Rich: Hill, Jr.	1
Thomas Bell	2	Obedience Johnson	3	Danll Etion	2
Alphansoe Ball	1	Jno. Goring	1	Robt: Richardson	2
Jno: Walthom	5	Benjamin Lawrence	1	Nath: Bradford	5
Nich: Lawrance	1	Alexandr Addison	5	Timothy Coe	3
Richard Kellum	6	Fulcot Obin	1	Stephen Barnes	1
Wm. Roberts	6	Mrs. Jordan	8	Robt. Watson	1
Jno. Savage	1	Jno. Pepper	1	Wm. Blake	1
Liveing Denwood	5	Jonah Jackson	3	Edward Hamon	3
Geo: Brickhouse	4	Donak Denis	1	Richard Smith	1
Jno. Haggaman	2	Phillip Fisher	4	Charles Russell	1
Jno. Thompson	2	Wm. Smith	3	Edward Dunston	2
John Evans	2	Edward Dolby	2	Majr. Jno. Tilney	11

In all 468 - v. i - p. 102

A List of Tithables in Accomack County A.D. 1666

Name	Tithes	Name	Tithes	Name	Tithes
Coll Edm: Scarburgh	33	Giles Cope	2	Mr. Devorax Browne	11
Wm. Major	4	Mr. Henry Smith	12	Henry White	2
Jonas Jackson	3	Ralph Dow	2	Thomas Smith	2
Jno. Smith	3	Jno. Shepheard	6	Jno. Turnor	3
Alexander Addison	6	Jno. Savage	1	Samuel Jones	2
Thomas Allygood	1	George Hamling	2	Jno. Goring	2

ACCOMACK TITHABLES (Tax Lists): 1663 - 1695

Name	Tithes	Name	Tithes	Name	Tithes
Edward Smith	3	Geo: Brickhouse	3	Samuell Showell	1
Wm. Roberts	4	Jno. Paramore	3	Edw: Hamon	3
Edward Moore	4	Major Tilney	8	Robt. Richardson	2
Arthur Upshott	3	Barth: Meers	1	Richard Smith	1
Richard Hill	1	Thomas Bell	2	Phillip Fisher	4
Wm. Smith	4	Nath: Bradford	5	Tho: Browne	4
Henry Edwards	3	Daniell Etion	2	Tho: Marvill	1
Morgan Dowell	4	Wm. Taylor	2	Jno. Tompson	3
Eliza. Rackliff	6	Henry Stott	1	James Camwell	1
Edward Dolby	2	Robert Brace	2	Benjamin Laurance	1
Tobius Sellvey	1	Henry Browne	2	Capt. Bowman	4
Robt. Watson	1	Jno. Willis	1	Mary Paramore	1
Jno. Eyres	2	Henry Bishopp	6	Wm. White	1
Tho: Selby	1	Robt. Bayley	2	Jno. Fawset	4
Dermon Selevant	3	Stephen Barnes	1	Robt. Hewitt	6
James Hinderson	2	Wm. Dine	2	Owen Collonon	2
Edw: Revell	4	Wm. Aborne	2	Henrick Able	2
Goodwife Millby	2	Daniell Ograhan	1	Tho: Hall	3
Mr. Fleming	2	Richard Kellum	6	Tho: Wingood	1
Danll Darby	1	Rowland Savage	1	Richard Niblet	1
Edward Sacker	2	Jno. Walthom	5	Geo: Johnson	3
Richard Bayley	5	Robt. Hutchinson	2	Rody Patrick	1
Thomas Osborne	1	Jno. Tike	2	Jno. Cropper	1
Andrew Finne	2	Richard Hill	7	Mrs. Charlton	1
David Williamson	5	Capt. West	6	Alphanso Ball	2
Thomas Fowke	5	Jno. Watts Sr.	2	Michill Ricketts	3
Walter Taylor	5	Francis Benston	3	Morris Denis	3
Jno. Drumon	3	Thomas Tunnell	3	Wm. Custis	4
Jno. Holding	1	Teage Andrews	3	Mrs. Hack	3
Alexander Massy	2	Xp: Calvert	2	Wm. Silverthorne	1
Mr. Littleton	6	Geo: Trewit	4	Edward Smally	2
Tho: Leatherberry	5	Anto. Longo	1	Wm. Onoughten	1
Wm. Chase	2	Jno. Jenkins	2	Richard Johnson	1
Jno. Watts	1	Jno. Brookes	1	James Bonwell	4
Richard Prichet	1	Jno. Wallop	3	Mr. Wise	7
Jno. Renny	4	James Fookes	6	Jno. Parker	6
Francis Sherwood	2	James Jolly	5	John Williams	6
Jno. Michaell	5	Van Nitsin	1	Wm. Benston	2
Mr. Hugh Yeo	8	Edw: Smith, Mill	gone		
Howell Glading	1	wright			
Mrs. Ann Toft	8	Tim. Coe	"		
Richard Bunduck	2	Jno. Lewis	"		
		Mr. Pitts	"		

In all 453 Tithables - v. ii - p. 35

A List of Tithables in Accomack County A.D. 1667

Name	Tithes	Name	Tithes	Name	Tithes
Coll Scarburgh	43	Wm. Ebourne	3	Richard Bayly	4
Tho: Tunnell	1	Robt. Hewit	4	Jno. Savage	1
Wm. White	1	Robt. Richardson	3	Danll. Selby	2
Owen Collonan	2	Jno. Le Cat	2	Dermon Selevant	3

ACCOMACK TITHABLES (Tax Lists): 1663 - 1695

Name	Tithes	Name	Tithes	Name	Tithes
Ab: Taylor	1	Michill Rickets	3	Wm. Dine	2
Rich: Hill	1	Jno. Marvill	1	Edw: Hitchin	1
Ja: Atkinson	1	Jno. Smith	2	Tho: Osborne	1
Jno. Fawset	4	Mr. Littleton	5	Rich: Kellum	6
Danll. Darby	2	Tho: Fowke	6	Tho: Hall	5
Jno. Turnon	3	Robt. Bayly	2	Tobius Sellvey	1
Henrick Waggaman	2	Rich: Buckland	1	Jno. Brookes	2
Mr. Yeo	8	Jno. Smally	2	Wm. Custis	3
Cornelius Watkinson	1	Morrice Dennis	3	Nath: Bradford	5
Wm. White, wheelrite	1	Xp: Calvert	2	Jno. Parker	4
Husalin Vannitsin	1	Jno. Jenkins	1	Howell Glading	1
Wm. Anderson	4	Wm. Chase	2	Tho: Leatherberry	4
Richard Johnson	1	Wonne Macktlamy	3	John Walthom	5
Geo: Truett	4	Mr. Bowman	7	Jno. Watts, Coop:	1
John Lewis	4	Tho: Wingood	1	Tho: Ovila	1
Laurance Robinson	1	Roger Turnon	1	Jno. Dix	3
Fenlow Maxwilliam	1	Tho: Bagwell	1	Jno. Carew	1
Wm. Burton	1	Jno. Arew	2	Mr. Wise	4
Wm. Gowers	2	Walter Taylor	4	Jno. Drumon	3
Capt. Parker	7	George Johnson	4	Widdow Bonwell	2
John Williams	3	Danll Ograhan	1	Francis Benston	2
Mrs. Ann Toft	16	Jno. Renny	3	John Watts	2
Wm. Benston	3	James Fookes	2	Jno. Wallop	4
Edw: Smith, Millwright	3	Robt. Houston	2	Rich: Bunduck	3
Edw: Sacker	2	Edw: Vaughan	1	Alex: Massy	1
Timothy Coe	3	Jno. Parker, taylor	1	Capt. Hill	5
Browne Herricks	2	Mr. Charles Scarburgh	7	Peter Walker	2
David Williamson	4	Teage Andrews	2	Wm. Silverthorne	1
Robt. Hutchinson	4	Mr. Edw: Revell	3	Abram Bucle	1
Nich: Tubbin	1	Henry White	1	Jno. Cobb	1
Edw: Dolby	2	Hen: Bishop	5	Wm. Major	3
Edw: Smith	3	Fulcot Obin	1	Tho: Jacob	2
Henry Browne	gone	Wm. Roberts	4	Jno. Paramore	2
Tho: Githing	1	Nicholas Laylor	2	George Brickhouse	3
Danll Etion	2	Wm. Tinsby	2	Jno. Burch	1
Jno. Goring	2	Thomas Smith	1	Jonah Jackson	4
Edmd. Kelly	3	Mary Paramore	2	Henry Stott	3
Ralph Dow	2	Jno. Michael	2	Thomas Browne	5
Jno. Shephard	6	Henry Smith	9	Edw: Hamon	3
Giles Cope	1	Robt. Watson	1	Edward Moore	3
Wm. Branchly	1	Major Jno. Tilney	8	Wm. Rapishare	2
Robert Blake	1	Thomas Alligood	1	Wm. Taylor	1
Jno. Tomson	3	Wm. Smith	3	Phillip Fisher	4
Alexander Adison	5	Geo. Hamlin	2	Rody Patrick	1
Samuell Jones	1	Tho: Marshall	3	James Camwell	2
Widdow Rackliff	5	Obedience Johnson	3	In all 442 and	

referred to James Towne. The 24 added at laying the Levie: Germon Gillit 1
    Mr. Jolly 1
    Mr. Nich: Boot 7

Capt. Pitt 4
v. ii - p. 60
    Mr. Devorax Browne 11

ACCOMACK TITHABLES (Tax Lists): 1663 - 1695

A list of Tithables in Accomack County A.D. 1668

Name	Tithes	Name	Tithes	Name	Tithes
Charles Rackliff	4	Jno. Bowan	2	Jno. Drumon	3
John Keeble	5	George Trewit	5	Francis Benston	4
Teage Miscall	1	Thomas Osbourne	)	Jno. Renny	3
James Taylor	1	John Higgs	) 2	Capt. Rich: Hill	5
Wm Blake	2	Walter Taylor	5	Jno. Lewis	4
Laurance Robinson	1	Fenlow Mackwilliam	1	Jno. Pike	2
Mr. Charles Scarburgh	6	David Williamson	3	Wm Gowers	3
Roger Mikeel	3	Roger Barter	2	Mr. James Fookes	2
John Cary	1	Joseph Newton	2	Roger Turnon	1
Mr. Jno. Parker	3	Thomas Riley	2	Wm. Anderson	1
Jarmon Gilliet	2	Jno. Parker, taylor	1	Robt. Sikes	1
Jno. Watts, Cooper	1	Morris Denis	3	David Dale	3
Timothy Coe	4	Wm Silverthorne	1	Jno. Wallop	2
Wm Benston	2	Rich: Bundock	4	Teage Anderson	2
Jno. Hepworth	2	Henrick Able	2	Edw: Smith	3
Mr. Jno. Michael	3	Jno. Sturgis	1	Mr. Jno. Wise	3
George Johnson	4	Tho: Shelleto	1	Edw: Moore	2
Mr. Tho: Leatherberry	4	Jno. Watts	2	Jno. Travally	1
Tho: Bowles	1	James Walker	3	Wm. Marshall	1
Jno. Jenkins	3	Peter Prichet	3	Alexandr Massy	1
Griffeth Savage	1	Ellias Anderson	1	Edw: Vaughan	2
Tho: Benthall	1	Wm Alworth	1	Robt. Hutchinson	5
Capt. Geo: Parker	6	John Savedge	1	Henry Forse	1
Coll Edm: Scarburgh	16	Mr. Tho: Fowke	5	Tho: Allygood	1
Rich: Hill junyr	1	Jno. Rickets	1	Edw: Hitchin	1
Mr. Nath: Bradford	5	Anto. Longo	1	Browne Henrick	2
Mr. Edw: Revell	3	Rich: Kellam	6	Mrs. Boate	5
Danll. Foxcroft	1	Michill Rickords	5	Jno. Walthom	4
Rich: Bayley	5	Jno. Fawset	6	Danll. Ograhan	1
Wm Taylor	2	Wm Wilson	1	Mr. Wm Custis	3
Rowland Savedge	1	Edw: Sacker	1	Jno. Holden	1
Wm Burton	3	Abraham Heath	1	Tho: Bagwell	2
Mr. Hugh Yeo	8	Danll. Darby	1	Jno. Marvell	1
Samll Showell	1	Edw: Smally	1	Tho: Hall	3
David Gibbins	1	Robt. Bayley	2	James Ewell	2
Tho: Tunnell	1	Wm Ebourne	2	Jno. Smally	1
Wm White	1	Henrick Wagaman	1	Robt. Bracy	1
Henry Wright	1	Barth: Meers	2	Rich: Johnson	1
Phillip Ockohaid	1	Wm Chase	3	Gilbert Skiner	2
Mr. Southy Littleton	3	Robt. Richardson	2	Mr. Jno. Smith	4
Tobias Selvey	3	Mr. Devorax Browne	12	Rich: Buckland	1
Dermon Selevant	3	Jno. Brookes	1	Owin Collen	2
Xp: Calvert	1	Abraham Taylor	1	Howell Glading	2
Robt. Hewitt	6	Rich: Niblet	2	Jno. LeCatt	1
Edw: Moore	2	Andrew Finne	1	Jno. White	1
Mr. Edw: Bowman	7	Geo: Brickhouse	4	Samll. Jones	2
Wm Rapishaw	4	Alex: Addison	5	Tho: Browne	5
Henry Stott	3	Jno. Goring	1	Danll. Etiam	2
Phillip Fisher	3	Jno. Jeames	1	Nich: Tubbin	1
Denis Selevant	1	Nich: Hudson	1	Nich: Laylor	2
Mary Paramore	2	Wm Major	5	Jno. Prittyman	1

ACCOMACK TITHABLES (Tax Lists): 1663 - 1695

	Tithes		Tithes		Tithes
Jno. Michael	2	Edw: Dolby	3	Wm Smith	4
Robt. Blaids	1	Jno. Truman	1	Tho: Jacob	3
Tho: Gittins	1	Edw: Hamon	2	Jno. Burt	1
Jno. Cuttin	1	Ralph Dow	1	Jno. Thomson	2
Jno. Evans	2	Geo: Hamling	2	Peter Doughty	2
Hen: Smith	7	Tho: Marshall	2	Geo: Dewy	2
James Camell	1	Jno. Paramore	2	Falcott Obin	1
Henry Bishop	3	Obedience Johnson	2	Jno. Hopkins	1
Jno. Pepper	1	Edw: Smith	2	Nich: Laurance	1
Jonah Jackson	3	Wm Roberts	4	Major Jno. Tilney	6
Wm Tildgly	1	Henry White	2	Morgan Dowell	2
Van Nitsin	2	Edm: Kelly	2	Jno. Walford	

Sum totall 458 returned to James Citty - v. ii - p. 80

A list of Tithables in Accomack County A.D. 1669

Coll Edm: Scarburgh)		John Tompson	2	Wm Smith	3
besids tradsmen)	19	Jno. Sanders	1	Jno. Burt	1
Jno. Trueman	1	Denis Selevant	2	Nich: Tubbin	2
Thomas Marshall	2	Robt. Watson	1	Alexander Addison	5
Obedience Johnson	3	George Hamling	3	Fulcot Obin	1
John Gording	1	Jno. White	1	Edmund Kelly	3
Jno. Hamerin	1	Danll Etion	2	Nicholas Laylor	1
Samuell Jones	2	Tho: Browne	6	Gusalin Vannetson	1
Jno. James	1	Giles Coope	2	Peter Clavill	1
Phillip Fisher	4	Jno. Cutten	1	John Paramore	3
Geo: Dewy	2	Jonah Jackson	4	Ralph Dow	1
Henry Bishop	3	Rich: Hinman	1	Edw: Smith	2
Jno. Michael	2	Mr. Hopkins	1	Mary Paramore	1
Jno. Evans	1	Wm Major	5	Jno. Prittyman	1
Nicholas Laurance	1	Henry Smith	7	Henry White	1
Major Jno. Tilney	6	Arthur Upshott	- 3	Edw: Hitching	1
Tho: Gittins	1	Richard Hill	1	Tho: Bell	1
Bartholomew Meeres	1	Wm Roberts	5	Daniell Darby	1
Henry Stott	1	Richard Smith	1	Jno. Dolby	1
Dormon Selevant	3	Geo: Brickhouse	3	Tobias Sellvey	1
Mrs Jordan	3	Jno. Smally	1	Edward Dolby	3
Jno. Barnett	1	John Golloe	1	Richard Kellam	4
Mr. Southy Littleton	4	Jno. Willis	1	Rich: Jones	1
Anto. Longo	1	Tho: Barton	1	Wm Walton	1
Francis Roberts	2	Jno. Brookes	1	Jno. Fawset	4
Howell Glading	3	Robt. Richardson	1	William Chase	4
Thomas Bowles	3	Mrs. Ann Boate	4	Mr. Hugh Yeo	8
Richard Buckland	1	Danll Ograhan	1	Wm Taylor	2
William Wilson	1	Daniell Foxcroft	1	John Cropper	2
Wm Ebourne	3	William Willowby	1	Tho: Fowke	4
Francis Benstone	2	Jno. Walthom	3	Robt. Huitt	6
Jno. Holding	1	John Rickards	2	Michill Rickards	3
Joseph Pitman	1	Henry Wright	1	Jno. Lecatt	1
Henrick Wagaman	1	Wm White	1	John Marvill	1
Robt. Hutchinson	4	Daniell Carter	1	Mr. Edw: Revell	2

ACCOMACK TITHABLES (Tax Lists): 1663 - 1695

Name	Tithes	Name	Tithes	Name	Tithes
Abraham Taylor	2	Mr. Jno. Wise	3	Rich: Bayley	5
Mr. Jno. Michael	3	James Ewell	2	Teage Anderson	1
Rich: Holland	1	Roger Mikeel	2	George Cutting	1
Wm Silverthorne	1	David Gibbins	1	Christopher Calvert	1
Tho: Tunnell	1	Jno. Pike	1	Peter Walker	1
David Williamson	2	John Savage	1	Jno. Jenkins	3
Edw: Haman	3	Tho: Leatherberry	3	Jno. Smith	2
Wm Benston	4	Edw: Smally	1	Elias Finah	1
John Watts, Cooper	3	Xp: Tompson	1	Henrick Able	1
Geo: Johnson	4	Jno. Parker	4	Morris Denis	3
Walter Taylor	5	James Taylor	1	Wm Anderson	2
Robt. Bracy	1	Joseph Newton	1	Jno. Lewis	5
James Fooke	2	Tho: Ryley	2	Robt. Hill	2
Roger Ternon	2	Alexander Massy	1	Fenlow Mackwilliam	1
Robt. Mason	1	Jno. Cary	1	Jno. Rowles	1
John Ayres	2	Jno. Parker, Taylor	1	Samuell Tomlinson	4
Elias Anderson	1	Capt. Rich: Hill	4	Nath: Bradford	5
Henry Chancy	1	Wm Burton	3	Morris Liston	4
Roger Kirkman	1	Wm Martin	1	Wm Custis	3
Wm Gray	1	Edw: Sacker	2	Edw: Smith	2
Tho: Bagwell	3	Jno. Watts	2	James Walker	1
Germon Gilliot	4	Phillip Quinton	1	Robt. Sikes	2
Grifeth Savedge	1	Jno. Renny	5	Capt. West	6
Edw: Vaughan	1	Mrs. Charlton	2	Timothy Coe	2
Capt. Geo: Parker	6	Rich: Bunduck	4	Wm Blake	3
Jno. Stockly	2	Geo: Truitt	3	Jno. Wallop	1
Charles Rackliff	3	Mrs. Ann Toft	21	Jno. Arew	2
Capt. Edm: Bowman	10	Francis Wharton	1	Jno. Hepworth	1
Teage Miscall	1	Jno. Drumon	4		

Sume Totall 454 - v. ii - p. 133

A list of Tithables in Accomack County A.D. 1670

Name	Tithes	Name	Tithes	Name	Tithes
Edward Moore	3	Jno: Watts	1	James Taylor	1
Hen: Permaine	2	Laurance Robinson	1	Rich: Bundock	2
John Lewis	3	Jno. Sturgis	2	Jno. Drumond	4
Rich: Johnson	1	Wonne Maclamme	2	Edw: Smally	1
Roger Turnon	1	Wm Kennet	1	Thomas Ryle	2
Timothy Coe	3	Jno. Arue	3	Mrs. Ann Toft	45
Jno. Ayres	3	Capt. Rich: Hill	5	Fenlow Mackwilliam	1
Joseph Newton	1	Francis Wharton	1	John Pike	1
Morris Denis	3	Ellias Finne	1	Rich: Marrinor	1
Teage Anderson	1	Geo: Johnson	3	Jno. Jenkins	3
Wm Marshall	1	Cristop: Calvert	3	Morris Liston	4
Alex Massy	2	Francis Benston	2	Wm Benston	3
Wm Onoughton	2	Abross White	3	Geo: Truet	4
Jno. Watts, Cooper	3	Tho: Midleton	2	Mr. Wise	6
Jno. Renny	6	Wm Anderson	1	Jno. Booin	3
Jno. Roles	1	Edw: Vaughan	2	Mr. Wm Custis	3
Charles Rackliff	3	Wm Jarmon	1	Jarmon Gilliot	4
Edward Sacker	2	Wm Lowin	1	Tho: Bagwell	2

ACCOMACK TITHABLES (Tax Lists): 1663 - 1695

	Tithes		Tithes		Tithes
Capt. Bowman	9	John Bagwell	3	James Powell	2
EdwL Smith	2	William Burton	4	Samuell Taylor	1
Tho: Leatherberry	2	Jno. Wallop	1	Rich: Pywell	1
Roger McKeel	3	Thomas Tunnell	2	Mr. Jno. Mickael	1
Mr. Jno. Smith	2	Wm Silverthorne	1	Francis Roberts	1
Mr. Jno. Parker	4	Edw: Hitchin	1	Walter Taylor	6
Nich: Tyler	1	Mr. James Fookes	2	Barth: Meeres	1
Jno. Fenn	1	Jno. Smally	1	Robert Hill	2
Jno. Brookes	1	Capt. Jno. West	10	Rich: Holland	1
Capt. Geo: Parker	8	Jno. Rickards	3	Coll Scarburgh	22
Jno. Willis	1	Mr. Southy Littleton	5	Rich: Bayley	5
Samll. Showell	2	Robt. Huet	6	Jno. Marvell	1
David James	1	Tho: Bushell	1	Wm White	1
Joseph Pitman	1	Jno. Walthom	3	Wm Willson	2
Owin Collonon	1	Edw: Hamon	3	Rich: Hill	1
Jno. Barnet	1	Tho: Fowke	5	Peter Prichet	1
Danll. Foxcroft	1	Jno. Savage	1	Robt. Mason	1
Howell Glading	3	Henry Wright	2	James Ewell	1
Mckiel Rickards	3	Wm Chase	2	Dorman Selevant	2
Danll. Clauson	1	Jno. Cropper	4	Wm Nock	2
Tobius Sellvey	1	Richard Kellam	3	Rich: Buckland	1
Jno. Lecat	1	Thomas Bowles	2	Rich: Niblet	1
Mrs. Charlton	2	Peter Walker	2	Wm Ebourne	2
Danll Ograhan	1	Jno. Fawset	3	Tho: Benthall	1
Danll. Darby	2	Geo: Collen	1	Wm Taylor	3
Jno. Booth	1	Mrs. Boate	4	Henry Stott	1
Jno. Holden	1	Gusalin Vanilson	2	Mr. Devorax Browne	16
Daniell Etiam	2	Wm Littlehouse	1	Gabrill Teage	2
Japhet Cooke	1	Jno. Hamerin	1	Mr. Hugh Yeo	7
Nich: Laylor	1	Nath: Bradford	6	Jno. Truman	2
James Atkinson	1	Denis Selevant	1	Roger Kirkman	1
Robt. Hutchinson	4	Ralph Dow	1	Mr. Edw: Revell	3
Peter Clavell	1	Tho: Marshall	2	Jno. Prittyman	2
Obedience Johnson	4	Wm Willoughbye	1	Jno. Gording	1
Wm Roberts	3	Jno. Cutting	2	Henry Chancee	2
Jno. Scanel	1	Wm. Major	2	Rich: Smith	1
Wm Rappishaw	1	Phillip Fisher	1	Mr. Tho: Browne	5
Hendrick Able	1	Tho: Bell	1	Edw: Dalby	2
Nicholas Laurance	1	Jno. Tompson	4	Tho: Paramore	2
Nich: Tubbin	2	Jno. Odobby	2	Rich: Southern	2
Phillip Jacob	3	Tho: Johnson	2	Samll Jones	3
Wm Smith	3	Alex: Addison	2	Geo: Brickhouse	3
Edm: Kelly	4	Thomas Barton	1	Jonah Jackson	2
Jno. Shepheard	9	Wm. Robinson	2	John White	1
Robt. Watson	1	Jno. Michael	3	Arthur Robins	3
Isaac Jacob	3	Fulcot Obin	1	Giles Cope	2
Jno. Goslee	1	Wm Williams	1	Major Jno. Tilney	6

Sume Total 518 - v. ii - p. 165

ACCOMACK TITHABLES (Tax Lists): 1663 - 1695

A list of the Tithables in the Upper part of Northampton County, A.D. 1671
Mr. Sowthy Littleton's List

Name	Tithes	Name	Tithes	Name	Tithes
Mr. Edward Revell	3	John Hutchinson	2	Henry Truett	2
John Cropper	5	Wm Chase	2	Hugh Partrige	1
Owin Collowell	2	Tobias Selbye	1	John Parker	3
Ralph Doe	1	Mrs. Anne Boot	5	John Brookes	2
James Ewell	1	John Goslin	1	Walter Taylor	6
Mr. Thomas Fowks	5	John Smalley	1	John Watts	1
John Holding	1	John Barnett	1	Thomas Reley	2
Jno. Perry	1	Roger Barton	1	Fenlaw MacWilliams	2
Mr. Sowthy Littleton	6	Thomas Bowles	1	Robt. Bruce	1
William Nock	2	Edmd. Scarburgh	2	Tho: Middleton	3
Hendrick Waggaman	1	Ambrose White	2	Edwd. Moor	1
Richd. Holland	1	Richd. Bayly	5	Wm Ayleworth	1
Elias Finne	1	John Willis	1	James Taylor	1
Richd. Niblet	1	John Ricketts	2	John Parker	1
Michaill Rickards	3	John Lecatt	1	John Lewis	5
Henry Selman	1	Abraham Taylor	2	Teage Anderson	2
Samll Shewell	1	John Fawsett	4	John Rew	2
Xpther: Mather	1	Nathll. Bradford	9	Roger Ternan	2
John Sheppard	9	Wm. Wilson	1	Joseph Newton	1
Dormon Sellevan	2	Robert Huett	6	Roger Mackeell	5
Danll Darby	1	Wm White	1	Wm Silverthorne	1
John White	1	Mr. Devorax Browne	14	Robert Hill	2
John Rolles	3	Howell Gladding	2	Richard Hill	5
Obedience Johnson	4	Francis Roberts	2	John Ayres	2
Tho: Johnson	2	Danll Cartee	2	Richd. Marriner	2
Wm. Major	2	James Adkinson	2	George Truett	1
Arthur Robins	4	Japhett Cook	2	John Drumond	3
Alexander Addison	6	Foulkett Obben	1	Richd. Pywell	2
John Smith	1	Edwd. Hammond	3	Xpher: Calvert	2
Thomas Marshall	2	Edwd. Hittchin	1	Wony Macglamen	1
John Goring	1	Edwd. Moore	1	John Cary	1
Edwd. Smalley	1	Robt. Hutchinson	4	Morris Dennis	3
Robert Mason	1	Mr. Hugh Yeo	7	Dennis Mores	1
Joseph Pittman	1	Bartholomew Meares	2	Timothy Coe	2
John Savage	2	Danll Ograhon	1	George Johnson	4
Richard Hall	1	Soubat Delstaties	1	Peter Prichd.	2
Edwd. Martin	1	Mrs. Charlton	2	Danll. Owen	1
Richd. Jefferyes	2	Arthur Upshott	3	James Fowkes	3
Thomas Parrimor	1	Humphry Jennings	2	Wm Benston	1
James Camell	1	Ann Boot for Jno.		Wm Andrewson	3
George Dewe	2	Wmson	1	Peter Walker	1
John Hamarin	1	Hugh Boyn	1	Richd. Hinman	1
Nicholas Laler	1	John Browne	1	Cornelius Verhoofe	1
John Smith	2	Emanll. a Portugall	1	Morris Liston	3
Robt. Watson	1	Darby Regon	1	Francis Benston	2
William Taylor	4	Richd. Sadbrook	1	Wm Browne	1
Wm Williams	2			Alexr. Massey	2
Richd. Kellum	3	Mr. John Wise his list		John Fen	2
Mathew Ship	2	Thomas Leatherberry	3	Mr. John Wise	4
Mrs. Walthum	2	John Jenkins	2	Majr. Geo: Parker	7

ACCOMACK TITHABLES (Tax Lists): 1663 - 1695

Name	Tithes	Name	Tithes
Thomas Willers	1	Goody Parramor	1
Wm Brittingham	2	Thomas Browne	6
Robt. Sikes	3	Nicholas Lawrence	1
Capt. Jno. West	10	John Thompson	3
Lawrence Robinson	1	Jno. Scannell	1
Xpher: Thompson	1	Jno. Cuttin	1
John Marvell	1	Edward Dolbye	2
Mr. Charles Scarburgh	9	John Coare	4
		Henry Stott	1
Capt. Bowman's List:		Hendrick Abell	1
German Gillett	5	Phillip Fisher	2
John Stockley	4	John Trewman	1
Wm Hickmer	2	Thomas Barton	1
Richd. Bundick	2	George Brickhouse	4
John Sturgis	1	John Prittiman	2
Wm Marshall	1	Wm Roberts	4
Thomas Lamkin	2	Van Nitzon	1
Wm Lowing	1	Emanll. Hall	1
Charles Ratcliff	5	Dennis Sullevan	1
Wm Kennett	1	Edmd. Kelly	4
Wm Collins	2	Thomas Bell	1
John Bagwell	2	Thomas Gittings	1
James Walker	1	Thomas Madox	2
Henry Williams	1	Nicholas Tubbin	2
Thomas Bagwell	4	John Burt	1
Francis Williams	1	John Dolbye at Mr.	
Richd. Franklin	1	Yeo's plantacon	1
Wm Walton	1	Fowke Evans	2
Wm Coslie	3		
Wm Burton	2	Sume 545 of Tithables - v. iv - p. 29	
Wm Card	2		
Edwd. Sacaker	3		
Capt. Edmd. Bowman	8		
Edwd. Smith	3		
Richd. Johnson	1		
Wm Blacke	1		
John Wallop	3		
Roger Kirkman	1		
John Wates	1		
Edwd. Vaughan	1		
Wm Crabtree	1		
Samll. Taylor	1		
Capt. Jenefer	11		
Miles Grey	1		
Coll Scarburgh	40		
Mr. Isack Foxcroft's List:			
John Michaell, Junr.	3		
Giles Copes	2		
Jno. Dolbye	1		
Lt. Coll Tilney	5		
Danll. Esham	2		
Wm Smith	3		

ACCOMACK TITHABLES (Tax Lists): 1663 - 1695

A List of Tithables in Accomack County A.D. 1674

	Tithes		Tithes		Tithes
Capt. Southy Littleton's List					
Capt. Southy Littleton	7	Roger Kirkman	1	Peter Watson	1
Japhett Cooke	1	Mrs. Tabitha Browne	14	Wm Blake	1
Mrs. Charlton	4	Mr. Hugh Yoe	6	Mr. Jno. Wise List	
Jno. Rust	1	Rich: Kellam, Sr.	5	Jno. Reney	3
Peter Morgan	1	Daniell Ograhon	1	Wiliam Waley	2
Morgan Thomas	1	Mr. Teakle hath 3 ser-		Samuel Stills	)
Jno. Holding	1	vants & for his other		Samuell Churchill	)3
Mathew Pope	2	3 allowed him by act		Geo: Sturges	)
Math: Shipp	2	of Assembly takes		Geo: West	2
Phill: Carter	1	Jno. Rowles, David		Denis Morris	1
Abra: Taylor	1	Gibons & William		Morris Denis	2
Daniell Darby	1	Elvin		Joseph Nuton	2
Owen Collonell	3	Thomas Russell	1	Robert Mill	2
Tobias Selvey	1	Jno. Harris	1	Teage Anderson	3
Ed: Scarburgh	6			Fenlow Mackwilliam	1
Rich: Jones sun &	)	Majr. Bowman's List		John Clerck	1
Robert Huetts	) 6	Mrs. Fowkes	2	William Willet	2
William White	1	Wm Morgan	1	Adam Robinson	1
Joseph Clerck	1	Rich: Johnson	2	Henry Trewet	1
John Lecatt	2	Henry Barnes	1	Wil: Silverthorne	1
Derman Swilliam	4	Samuell Tayler	1	Will: Anderson	2
Rich: Bayley	8	Robert Atkins	1	Thomas Fooks	1
Samuell Serjant	1	John Sturges	1	Vincent Oliver	1
Danell Mackarty	1	John Bowen &	)	John Lewis	3
Rowland Savage	2	William Stockly	) 2	Roger Miles	1
John Gozoling	1	Peter Walker	1	Roger Mickell	6
Rich: Niblett	1	Isaac Dix	3	John Parker	5
Jno. Waltham	2	Wm Kennet	3	Will: Anaughton	2
James Atkison	2	Jno. Francisco	1	Richard Piwell	1
George Gin	2	Wm Morris	1	Jno. Jinkins	2
Jno. Cropper	4	Charles Ratcliffe	4	Rich: Hinman	1
Rhode Fawset	4	Wm Marshall	3	Francis Wharton	1
Henrick Waggaman	1	Robert Mason	1	William Grarman	2
Arthur Frame	1	Xtopher Stanly	1	Robert Davis	1
Robert Hutchinson	7	Will: Stockly	1	Robert Dungworth	1
John Coale	3	Mr. Wallop	4	George Truet	2
Daniell Cowen	1	Rich: Bundock, Senr.	2	John Ayres	3
Wm Chase	2	Will: Hickman	2	Xtopher Tomson	1
Thomas Bowles	2	Woodman Stockly	1	Thomas Riley	1
Henry Read	1	Will: Tayler, Senr.	3	Roger Ternall	1
Mrs. Boate	5	Edm: Bowman	9	Owen Macklanen	1
John Macomb	1	Edward Smith	4	John Rew	1
Darby Regon	1	Jno. Stratton	2	Capt. Rich: Hill	4
Rich. Hill Junr.	3	Guslin Venetson	1	Jno. Drummond	2
Edward Dale	1	Edw: Vahan	2	Phill: Hamon	1
Rich Jones Sr.	1	Nich: Millichop	1	Robert Watson	1
Lawrence Gery	1	Wm Lowing	1	Paul Carter	1
Jno. Kellam	1	Jno. Tayler at	)	Tho: Smalpec	1
John Smalle	1	Xtopher Stanleys	) 1	Jarman Gillet	2
Howell Gladding	1	Jno. Alore	1	Will: Brittingham	3

ACCOMACK TITHABLES (Tax Lists): 1663 - 1695

Name	Tithes	Name	Tithes	Name	Tithes
Will: Aleworth	2	Jno. White	1	Henry Lurtin	1
James Tayler	1	George Dowy	1	Jno. Burch	2
Alex: Marcy	2	Nich: Lalor	1	Nich: Tubbin	2
Francis Benston	1	Ralph Doe	1	Emanuell Hall	1
Teage Miskell	2	Jno. Henimin	1	John Thomson	4
George Johnson	6	Roger Baker	1	Mrs. Smith, widdow	3
Timothy Coe	2	Edward Wheatmost	1	Tho: Ryding	5
Robert Brace	1	Nicholas Lawrence	1	Tho: Robinson	2
Jno. Marvel	1	Jonah Jackson	3	Isaac Jacob	4
John Fen	2	Allex Addison	2		
John Gonsaloes	1	Jno. Booth	2	Capt. Wm Custis List:	
Peter Claver	1	Jo9hn Sheppard	6	John Bagwell	3
Joshua Smith	1	Robert Watson	1	Bartho: Meers	3
Will: Browne	1	Edw: More	1	William Cord	2
Jno. Cary	1	Arthur Robins	5	Jno. Barnes	4
the widdow Letherburies	4	Henry Chancey	2	Jno. Parker, Tayler	4
Peter Prichard	2	Edward Joyne	1	James Walker	1
Cornellus Verhoofe	1	Fra: Roberts	1	Henry Williams	3
Mrs. Brownes at Pokamock	3	Jno. Savidge	2	Jno. Willis	1
ditto at Deepe Creek	2	Wm Williams	1	William Burton	3
Thomas Nixson	3	Jno. Smith	3	Tho: Bagwell	2
Robert Spencer	1	Jno. Dolby	2	William Nock	2
John Tounson	1	Jno. Michaell	3	Edward Hichin	1
John Blokson	1	Henry Stott	1	James Ewell	1
Griffith Savage	2	Tho: Barton	1	Capt. Hen: Custis	2
Jno. Watts, Cooper	1	Samuell Glew	2	Nath: Bradford	10
James Fooke	4	Jno. Core	3	Edward Revell	5
Jno. Brouxe	3	Jno. Greene	1	Rich: Sheale)Mr.	
att Eliz: Robinsons		Jno. Cobb	1	Jno. Barnet)Upshars	3
Jno. Betts	1	Will: Abraham	1	Rich: Costin)	
Capt. Jno. West	9	Tho: Marshall	1	Rich: Franklin	1
Will: Davis	1	Law: Teage	1	Samuell Beech	2
Rich: Cutler	1	Giles Cope	2	Henry Pearmain	1
Mr. Jno. Wise	5	Elias Alexander "garganus"	1	Ambross White	4
Jno. Evens	2	Jno. Truman	1	William Freeman	1
Jno. Tayler	3	Tho: Browne	4	Edward Hamon	4
Phill: Ockahone	4	Geo: Brighouse	3	Capt. Daniell Jenifer	
Mrs. Florence Parker	6	Jno: Pritteman	2		38
Jno. _____?	1	James Harison	1	622 totall	
Canutus Bence	1	Jno. Tylney	5		
Edw: Brotherton	2	Phillip Fisher	2	A List of Delinquents	
Tho: Tayler	1	Denis Selivant	1	Jno. Longo	1
Mr. Charles Scarburgh	8	Thomas Gittins	1	Sam: Adkinson	1
Mr. Tho: Ryding's List:		Jeptha Johnson	1	Edw: Kellum	2
Jno. Gordian	2	Edm: Kelley	2	John Parkes	1
Obedience Johhnson	4	Tho: Maddox	1	Robert Peell	1
Jo: Pitman	1	Gabriell Teage	1	Jno. Renney's 2 boys	2
Thomas Johnson	2	Ed: Dolby	1	Jno. Jenkins 2 sons	2
Wm Major)	3	David James	1	Wheler att John	
Peter Dolby	3	Daniell Esham	2	Parkers one Boy	1
Thomas Parmor	2	Tho: Bell	5	Mrs Letherburys)	
James Scancll	1	Jno: Camell	1	son & negro)	2
Jno. Smith	1	Jno. Cuttin	2	Doller	

ACCOMACK TITHABLES (Tax Lists): 1663 - 1695

	Tithes
Majr. West 2 Indians	2
Mr. Wise an Ind:	1
Wm Smith, slopeman	1
Thos: Thomas	1
Mrs Parker one Indian George	1
Capt. Cha: Scarburgh) two Indians)	2
Jno. Straton 1 Indian to ye admistrs. att) ye tanhouse belong) ing to ye Estate) of Coll Scarburgh)	1 4
Nath: Bradford 1 Ind.	1
Capt. Hill 1 Ind.) called Dick)	1
Mr. Jno. Culpeper	1

Sume 651 tithables - v. v - p. 194

A List of Tythables in Accomack County A.D. 1675

	Tithes		Tithes		Tithes
Capt. Southy Littleton his List		Tob: Selvey	1	George Hope	1
		Wm Fletcher	3	Jno. Drumond	3
Capt. Southy Littleton	5	Robt. Huets	5	Roger Mikeel	6
Wm Chace	3	Wm White	1	Jno. Consalues	1
Geo: Nick: Hack	6	Tho: Barnet	2	Wm Silverthorne	1
Peter Yorke	3	Rich: Hill, Jr	1	Robt. Hill	1
Phillip Carter	1	Jno. Lecat	3	Jno. Carter	2
Rich: Niblet	1	Jno. Harris	2	Joseph Newton	2
Mathew Shipp	1	Abraham Tayler	1	Peter Prichard	2
Jno. Rowles	3	Joseph Clarke	1	Savat: Delastetious	1
Mathew Pope	1	Jno. Coale	5	Jno. Fen	3
Henry Belcher	1	Jno. Cutting	5	Tho: Fowkes	1
Robt: Hutchinson	7	Jno. Barnet	1	Rich: Piwell	1
Morgan Thomas	1	Henry Reade	2	James Natane	1
Jno. Holding	1	Rowland Savage	2	Jno. Marrien	1
Rich: Holland	1	Henry Selman	1	Mr. James Matts	7
Jno. Rust	1	Jno. Smally	1	Robt. Mason	1
George Charnock	1	Mrs. Charlton	3	Teage Andrews	3
Jno. Goodman	1	Roger Lerkman	1	Paule Carter	1
Wm. White	1	Mr. Hugh Yeo	10	Wm Anderson	3
Jno. Dyee	1	Danl. Ograhon	1	Jno. Watts	1
Own. Collonell	1	Mr. Teakles Tythables by the law allowes him & he enters ye other	3	Jno. Jenkins	5
Arnold Harrison	1			Tho: Tayler	1
Tho: Pinfold	1			Jno. Jones	1
James Atkison	1			Rich: Cutler	1
Tho: Tiron	1	Rhenny Sadler	1	Mr. Jno. Wise	7
Saml1. Atkison	1			Jno. Ayres	3
Wm Littlehouse	1	Mr. Jno. Wise List		Jno. Arew	1
Mrs. Browne) Tythables att Nandua)	11	Jno. Parker of Matapany	5	Wm Browne	1
				Mr. James Focks	5

14

ACCOMACK TITHABLES (Tax Lists): 1663 - 1695

	Tithes		Tithes		Tithes
Capt. Cha: Scarburgh	13	Rich: Bundick	2	Jno. Johnson	1
Tho: Webb	1	Jno. Sturges	2	Jno. Withum	2
Maj. Jno. West	15	Bartho: Meeres	5	Jno. White	1
Jno. Tayler	3	Edwd. Hitchin	1	Rhody Fawset	3
Wm Smith	1	Rich: Garretson	1	Obed: Johnson	4
Mrs. Leatherbury	3	Edwd. Hamond	4	Jno. Gording	2
Jno. Travally	1	Cha: Ratcliffe	4	Joseph Pittman	1
Wm Wilson	1	Danl. Owen	1	Tho: Marshall	1
Tho: Welborne	)	Saml. Beech	1	Jno. Smith	1
Hugh Welborne	) 3	Amb: White	6	Ralph Dow	2
Wm Sill	)	Rich: Hill	3	Japht. Cooke	2
		Edwd. Smith	5	Jno. Hamering	1
Capt. Wm Custis List		Wm Blake	2	Jno. Parks	1
Jno. Barnet	4	Wm Taylor, Jr.	3	Capt Edmd Scarburgh	8
Tho: Bagwell	2	Nathan: Bradford	9	James Camell	1
Wm Freeman	1	Tim: Tayler	2	Dorothy Jordan	3
Roger Miles	1	Maj: Ed: Bowman	11		
Rich: Jonson, Sr	2	Jno. Jackson	1	Mr. Tho: Ridings List	
Henry Williams	3	Capt. Danl. Jenifer)		Jno. Sheppard	4
Jno. Bagwell	3	number of Tyth-)	40	Tho: Brown	5
Robt. Dungwood	1	ables)		Jno. Burch	1
James Walker	2			Wm Lingo	1
Edward Revell	5	Capt. Edmd. Scarburgh		Mikl. Garding	1
Wm Burton	2	List		Jno. Mikeel	2
Isaack Medcalfe	2	Arthur Robins	5	Jno. Green	3
Wm Benston	2	Tho: Barton	1	Denes Selvent	1
Jonath: Owen	2	Wm Major	3	Tho: Bell, Jr	4
Capt. Wm Custis	2	Jno. Smith	4	George Brickhouse	4
Nicholas Millechop	5	Jno. Savage	3	Henry Scott	1
Jno. Bowen	4	Frans. Robins	2	Phil: Fisher	2
Peter Walker	1	Saml. Serjeant	1	Lawr. Teage	1
Jno. Wallop	5	Jno. Cropier	4	Amanl. Hall	1
Jno. Willis	1	Jno. Macome	1	Tho: Gittings	1
Robt. Mason	4	George Ginn	1	Isaac Jacob	3
Wm Nock	2	Alex: Addison	4	Jno. Prettiman, Sr	4
Henry Chancy	3	Jno. Booth	2	Tho: Glew	2
Wood: Stockely	1	George Dewey	1	Tho: Madox	4
Edmd. Allin	1	Edmd: Ginee	1	Jno. Truman	2
Wm Parker	3	Roger Barton	2	Jno. Thomson	4
Mrs. Fowkes	3	Giles Coop	2	Danl. Essam	2
James Ewell	1	Tho: Johnson	2	Jona. Core	3
Jno. Hanning	1	Jonas Jackson	4	Armstrong Foster	2
Henry Pairdmame	1	Richd. Kellum	4	Jno. Tankark	1
George Row	1	Nicholas Layler	1	Jno. Cuttin	2
Robt. Atkins	1	Jno. Kellum	1	Henry Lurton	1
Peter Watson	1	Wm Williams	2	Jno. Scamel	1
Jno. Watts	1	Robt. Watson	2	David James	1
Christ: Stannly	1	Dorm: Sullivan	3	Edwd. Dolby	1
Edwd. Vahan	1	Steph: Whittman	1	Edmd. Kelly	2
Van Etsan	1	Robt. Hodson	1	Jno. Snow	1
Rich: Franklin	1	Danl. Derby	1	Jeptha Johnson	1
Jno. Stratton	5	Derby Regon	1	Morgn. -----	3
Wm Revel	3	Tho: Parremore	4	Jno. Tilney	2

ACCOMACK TITHABLES (Tax Lists): 1663 - 1695

Name	Tithes	Name	Tithes	Name	Tithes
Tho: Riding	5	Rich: Hinman	1		
Mary Parremore	3	Jno. Blockson	1		
		Wm Lowen	1		
Capt. Rich: Hill's List		Jno. ----ounson	1		
George West	1	Teage Mickell	1		
Roger Freeman	1	Saml. Cutchkill	1		
Ong: Maclonny	1	Jno. Renny	4		
Fenlo Mackwilliams	1	Tho: Middleton	2		
Josua. Smith	1	Jno. Melson	1		
Jno. Cary	1	Jno. Price	1		
Wm Brittingham	3	Wm Onaught	1		
Tho: Natbolt	2	Amos Cooke	1		
Jerm: Jillit	2	Morrs. Dennis	2		
James Tayler	2	Robt. Bracy	1		
Alex: Marcy	2	Capt. Richd. Hill	7		
Frans. Benston	1				
Jno. Francisco	2	The Sume of Tythables is 702 - v. v -p. 325			
Wm Morris	1				
Geo: Midleton	2				
Tho: Barrit	1	A List of Tythables in Accomack County			
Isaac Dix	3	A.D. 1676			
Jno. Lewis, Sr	3				
Saml. Oliver	1	Jno. Cropper	4	Samuel Serjeant	1
Tho: Ryle	2	Mathew Shipp	1	Tho: Hall	3
Jno. Webster	2	Japhet Cooke	1	Wm Major	3
Abra: Dorton	1	Mr. Tho: Teakle	9	Jno. Harris	2
Jno. Brakes	3	Tho: Benthall	1	Arthr. Robins	5
Wm Hudson	1	Joseph Ames	1	Jno. Kellum	1
Corn: Bencha	1	Owen Collenon	5	Max: Gore	1
Jno. Evans	1	Danl. Darby	1	James Longo	1
Henry Truit	1	Wm Fletcher	3	Coll: So: Littleton	
Jno. Backe	1	Tobias Selvy	1		11
Dens. Morris	1	Jno. Cole	3	Jno. Smally	1
Jno. Bele	1	Jno. Nelson	2	Jno. Macome	1
Geo: Wheeler	2	Wm White	3	Mr. Richard Bally	6
Wm Garmon	1	Rowland Savage	2	Abraham Tayler	1
George Truit	1	Wm Williams	1	George Charnock	2
Peter Clavel	1	Wm Jones	1	Jno. Rust	1
Fran: Wharton	1	Morgan Thomas	2	Wm Wouldhave	1
Robt. Spencer	1	Tho: Tryar	1	Henry Selman	2
Robt. Davis	1	Richard Holland	1	Stephan Whittman	1
Grift. Savage	3	Edward Martin	1	Capt. Edmd. Scarburgh	
Wm Ailworth	2	Mrs. Fauset	3		5
Frans. Persons	2	George Ginn	1	James Atkins	1
George Johnson	6	Tho: Willson	1	Richard Kellum	6
Jno. Batta	1	James Steavens	1	Jno. Rowles	1
Tho: Smally	1	Edward Bird	1	Joseph Clarke	1
Jno. Evans	1	Robt. Hudson	--	Tho: Johnson	3
Howl. Glading	1	Dormt. Sellevant	4	Joseph Pittman	2
Jno. Franklin	3	Rich: Hill	1	Jno. White	1
Jno. Onion	4	Henry Reade	3	Jno. Barnet	1
Phill: Occahon	4	Jno. Lenham	1	Mr. Charlton	3
Tim: Coe	2	Robt. Huit	5	Roger Kerkman	1

ACCOMACK TITHABLES (Tax Lists): 1663 - 1695

Name	Tithes	Name	Tithes	Name	Tithes
David Gibbons	1	Mr. Robt. Hutchinson	7	Wm White	1
Jno. Feild	3	Rich: Niblet	1	Mr. Geo: Nich: Hack	5
Jno. Lecatt	--	Andrew Cornelison	1	Wm Dyne	1
Peter Yorke	1	Hend: Waggaman	2	Mrs. Tabitha Browne	
Francis Roberts	2	Rich: Welch	1		16
Jno. Parks	1	Alexdr. Addison	3	Jno. Booth	2
Jonha Jackson	3	Jno. Savadge	2	Jno. Smith	4
Wm Cobb	2	Robt. Watson	2	Nich: Layler	3
Jno. Hamering	1	Danl. Esham	1	George Duy	2
Isaack Jacob	2	Ralph Doe	3	Jno. Sheppard	5
Tho: Parremore	5	Jno. Goreing	2	Tho: Marshall	1
Jno. Smith	1	Mr. Tho: Browne	4	Jno. Corr	4
Rich: Sheale	3	Phill: Fisher	2	Tho: Gittings	1
Tho: Barton	1	Tho: Maddux	2	Jno. Truman	1
Tho: Bell, Jr.	4	Henry Scot	1	Munston Foster	1
Wm Yeo	3	Daniel Byles	1	Emanuel Hall	1
Edmd. Bowman	10	Jno. Burt	2	Redrick Powell	1
Wm Custis	2	Dennis Sellivant	1	Wm Nock	3
Mr. Wm Anderson	7	Tho: Savage	1	Jno. Willis	1
Jon. Parker of Mata:	6	David James	2	Rich: Holland	2
Wm Silverthorne	1	Wm Alby	3	Henry Chancy	2
Jno. Fenn	2	Edmd. Kelly	4	Mr. Edward Revell	6
Wm Willson	1	Jeptha Johnson	2	Richard Franklin	1
Rich: Cutler	1	Lt. Coll. Jno. Tilney	6	Garret Supple	2
Jno. Stokely, Sr	1	Georg Brickhouse	5	Darby Regon	1
Jno. Jenkins	5	Henry Stott	1	Henry Williams	2
James Bonewell	2	Laurence Atteage	1	Wm Burton	4
Stephen Warrington	2	Jno. Dolby	2	James Walker	1
Teage Andrewes	4	Tho: Bagwell	3	Robt. Hill	1
Giles Cope	2	Danl. Owen	2	Peter Prichard	2
Jno. Prettiman, Jr	1	Jno. Bagwell	3	Rich: Piwell	2
Nich: Laurence	1	Tho: Monford	1	Paul Carter	2
Henry Bramble	1	Edm: Allen	2	Mr. James Matts	7
Wm Whright	1	Barth: Meeres	4	Mr. James Tuck	1
Saml. Glew	2	Edward Hichin	1	Andrew Stott	1
Edmond Joynes	1	Wm Martiall	1	Jno. Lewis	1
George Smith	1	Peter Parker	2	Jno. Watts	1
Jno. Thomson	3	Robt. Watson, Sr	1	Jno. Tayler	3
Mr. Obedience Johnson	4	Nath: Bradford	9	Jno. Barks	1
Jno. Scamell	1	Wm Parker	1	James Fowkes	4
Nich: Tubbins man	1	Isaack Medcalfe	3	Joseph Nuton	2
Wm Cutting	1	Christopher Sadbury	1	Rich: Law	1
Henry Lurton	1	Jno. Gonsaloos	1	Richard Painter	2
Mr. Jno. Mickell	3	Rich: Garritson	1	Jno. Greene	1
Edward Hamond	5	Tho: Tayler	1	Edward Dolby	1
Wm Traffick	2	Roger Mikell	4	Roger Barker	3
Martin Oates	3	Jno. Wise, Sr	9	Jno. Read	1
James Ewell	1	Jacob Jregory	1	Mr. Tho: Ryding	4
Wm Freeman	1	A negro Woman in dispute		Widdow Parramore	3
Owen Daniel	1			Robt. Peale	1
Capt. Charles Scarburgh	9	Amb: White	7	Saml. Oliver	2
Jno. Parsons	2	Jno. Jones	1	Wonni Macklame	2
Jonathen Owen	2	Roger Ternham	2	Jno. Stockely	6

ACCOMACK TITHABLES (Tax Lists): 1663 - 1695

Name	Tithes	Name	Tithes	Name	Tithes
Edm: Bowman, Onancok	3	Maj. Jno. West	14	Arth: Frame	1
Wm Kennet	3	Mrs. Mary Scarburgh	2	George Midleton	1
Jno. Bowen	--	Xophr. Calvert son		Tho: Blacklock, Sr	2
Wm Blake	2	Charles	1	Tho: Webb	1
Jno. Lawes, Sr	4	Wm Brightingham	3	Rich: Bundock	3
Jno. Ares	2	Tho: Clifton	2	Rich Bundock, Sr	2
Chr. Thomson	1	Jno. Francisco, negro	2	Robt. Burton	2
Robt. Davis	1	Woodman Stokely	2	Jno. Tounsen	1
Wm Browne	1	Wm Stokely	1	Fran: Wharton	2
Jno. Marvill	1	Edward Wright	1	Rich: Hinman	1
Peter Clavill	2	Wm Prettiman	1	George Truit	1
Henry Armestrong	1	Wm Hickman	1	Nath: Fatherly	2
Wm Benston	1	Henry Truit	1	Jno. Hancock, Jr	3
Peter Morgan	1	Griffin Savage	3	Jno. Sturges	2
Tho: Perret	1	Jno. Abut	1	Rich: Johnson, Sr	2
George West	1	Wm Ailworth	1	Robt. Mason	5
Wm Lowen	1	Robt. Bracy	1	Jno. Cary	1
Henry Rodgers	1	Howel Glading	1	Jno. Arue	1
Jno. Watts	1	Jno. Carter	3	Morris Dennis	2
Jno. Renny	3	Adam: Robinson	1	Dennis Morris	1
Jno. Nelson	1	Jno. Brocks	4	Josua Smith	1
Gueslin Vannelson	2	Edward Carter	4	Timothy Coe	3
Finlow Mackwilliam	--	Jno. Onyons	4	Capt Danl Jenifer	26
Roger Miles	1	Isack Dix	1	Jno. Bloxum	1
Teage Mickell	1	Tho: Black	6	Tho: Smally	1
Wm Jarman	1	Wm Taylor, Sr	5	Wm Norton	1
Robt. West	1	Peter Walker	1	Jno. Evans	1
James Trewet	1	Evan Davis	1	Simond Smith	1
George Wheeler	1	Edw: Vahun	1	Tho: Nubold	4
Edward Breaderton	1	Nicho: Millechop	3	Saml. Crichill	1
Mr. Jno. Wallop	8	Charles Ratclift	3	Jno. Parsons	2
Samul. Taylor	3	Jno. Drumond	4	Xopher Stanly	2

736 Tythables in all - v. vii - p. 32

A List of the Tithables in Accomack County A.D. 1677

Name	Tithes	Name	Tithes	Name	Tithes
Capt. Wm Custis his List		Hillary Stringer	1	Ellias Garganis	1
		Jno. Jones	3	James Uell	1
Edward Revell	4	Tho: Bagwell	2	Henry Chancy	1
Jno. Stokely, Sr	1	Jno. Terry	1	Amb: White	10
Wm Burton	5	Rich: Franklin	1	To: Tayler	1
Tho: Mounford	1	Samuel Beech	2		
Wm Custis	6	Tabitha Browne	19	Mr. Jno. Wise List:	
Wm Nock	4	Wm Trafford	2	Jno. Fenn	2
Jno. Willis	1	Nath: Bradford	11	Tho: Fowkes	2
Henry Williams	2	Barth: Meares	4	Teage Anderson	4
James Walker	1	Tho: Clarke	1	Jno. Jenkins, Sr.	4
Jno. Bagwell	3	Rich: Costen	1	Steph: Warren	1
Jno. Bushop	2	Arth: Gaul	1	James Matts	9
Ed: Allen	1	Mart Otters	1	Wm Silverthorne	1
Isaack Medcalfe	1	Chris: Sadbury	1	Wm Willson	1

ACCOMACK TITHABLES (Tax Lists): 1663 - 1695

Name	Tithes	Name	Tithes	Name	Tithes
Tho: Burrowes	1	Wm Browne	1	Jno. Stokely	2
Jno. Parker	8	George West	1	Petr. Watson	1
Wm Anderson	7	Jno. Tounsend	1	Tho: Osburne	4
Jno. Lawes	1	Robt. Burton	1	Petr. Walker	1
Jno. Atkins	1	Paptis Nucomb	2	Jno. Tarr	1
Robt. Watson	1	Jno. Prettiman	3	Wm Tayler, Sr	9
Rich: Cutler	1	Wm Aillworth	2	Jonothn. Owen	2
Phill: Quinton	1	Teage Miskell	1	Jno. Bowen	4
Peter Prichard	2	Howel Glading	2	Max: Gore	3
Garret Supple	1	Tho: Basent	1	Jno. Moore	1
Joseph Nuton	1	Jno. Lewis, Sr	3	Jno. Watts	2
Tho: Morris	1	Jno. Brookes	3	Wm Stokely	2
Paul Carter	1	Jno. Parsons	3	Robt. Atkinson	1
Charles Leatherbury	4	Frans. Wharton	2	------Venetson	2
Jno. Lewis	1	Griff: Savage	2	Saml. Tayler	3
James Fowkes	3	Edward Brotherton	2	James Tayler	1
Roger Mikell	5	Roger Ternon	2	Allexdr. Massy	1
Darby Regan	1	Tho: Ryly	2	Cornutas Bence	1
Charles Calvert	2	Wm Thorton	1	Warrn. Harde	1
Jno. Tayler	1	Arthur Frame	1	Wm Brightingham	3
Jno. Gonsolvoe	1	Wm Wallis	2	Wm Benston	2
Andrew Stopp	1	Jno. Young	1	Tho: Barrit	1
Jno. Watts	2	Jno. Evan	1	Wm Blake	1
Robt. Hill	2	Jno. Millson	1	Wm Kennet	1
Jno. Wise	12	Jno. Renny	4	Tho: Clifton	1
Charles Scarburgh	9	James Booth	1	Jno. Francisco	1
Stephan Phillby	1	Onny Mackclamny	2	Hen: Rogers	1
Jno. West	15	Christopher Thomson	1	Xopr. Stanly	2
Tho: Webb	1	Tob: Bull	1	Tho: Nubold	4
Wm Anoughton	1	George Truit	2	Edwd. Rahan	1
Walter Tayler	1	Rich: Hinman	2	Petr. Morgin	1
		Dennis Morris	1	Roger Miles	1
Maj. Bowman's List		Wm Germane	3	Nich: Millechop	3
Wm White	3	Tho: Nixson	3	Rich: Williams	1
Rich: Bundick	2	Jno. Barnes	2	Evan Davis	2
Isaack Dix	2	Finlow Mackwilliams	1	Jno. Barke	1
Robt. Mason	5	Jno. Marvell	1		
Edmd. Bowman	12	Joshua Smith	1	Capt. Ed. Scarburgh:	
Jno. Sturgis	2	George Johnson	4	Owen Collonen	6
Rich: Johnson, Sr	2	Xophr. Roberts	2	Jno. Walthom	3
Wm Martiall	1	Robt. Dugins	1	Dormt. Sullivant	3
Wm Parker	1	Tho: Smalpeece	1	Rich: Holland	1
Peter Parker	2	Jno. Drumond	3	Morgen Thomas	3
Jno. Hancock	2	Richard Hill	6	Jno. Macome	1
Rich: Bundick, Jr	2	Timo: Coe	4	Richard Niblet	1
Jno. Hanning	1			Wm Symmont	1
		Mr. Jno. Wallop		Joseph Clarke	1
Capt. Hill's List		Jno. Wallop	11	Wm Dine	1
George Midleton	4	Danl. Jenifer	24	Michal Huit	6
Jno. Faree	1	Wood: Stokely	2	Tho: Hedges	1
Jno. Aierew	2	Nath: Ratclift	2	Edwd. Hichin	1
Peter Clavill	1	Rich: Hasting	1	Richard Hill	1
Jno. Abut	1	Jno. Stratton	1	Clemt. Onely	1

ACCOMACK TITHABLES (Tax Lists): 1663 - 1695

	Tithes		Tithes		Tithes
Wm Wouldhave	1	Tho: Barton	1	Jno. Parkes	1
David Gibbons	1	David James	2	Edmd. Joynes	1
George Charnock	1	Danl. Esham	1	Rich: Garrison	1
Jno. Goodman	1	Jno. Devenish	1	Arthr. Robins	5
Jno. Holden	1	George Bell	1	Jno. Smith, Sr	4
Row: Savage	3	Xophr. Maddex	1	Allexdr. Addison	4
Geo: Nich: Hack	5	Jno. Truman	1	Jno. Gordin	2
Tob: Selvy	2	George Brickhouse	4	Obed: Johnson	5
Henry Sellman	1	Henry Stott	1	Simon Foscue	2
Tho: Barnet	1	Vrmston Foster	1	Fras. Roberts	4
Wm Chace	3	Lau: Meage	1	Tho: Chapwell	2
Jno. Rowles	1	Wm Yeo	3	Ed: Moore, Sr	2
Ann Charlton	3	Morg: Weines	1	Wm Williams	1
Math: Shipp	1	Jno. Dolby	1	Rich: Welch	1
Rich: Bally	6	Jno. Mikell, Jr	4	Jno. Booth	2
Tho: Williams	1	Jno. Green	4	Jno. Smith, Jr	1
Mordy: Edwards	1	Dennis Selivant	2	Tho: Marshall	1
Robt. Hudson	1	Henry Lurton	1	Robt. Watson, Sr	4
Jno. Nellson	1	Eml. Hall	2		
Danl. Darby	1	Wm Cuttin	1	786 Totall -	
Nich: Tyler	1	Jno. Scamell	1		
Rich: Kellum	5	Jno. Johnson	1	v. vii - p. 56	
George Ginn	1	Rich: Melton	2		
Rhed: Powell	1	George Roe	1		
Tho: Bushell	1	Rich: Wood	1		
Edwd. Burd	1	Edmd. Kelly	4		
Jno. Millby	1	Nich: Tubbins	3		
Wm Major	4	Morg: Dewells	3		
Saml Serjeant	1	Jeptha Johnson	2		
Wm White	1	Jno. Tillny	4		
Jno. Lecat	2	Jno. Core	4		
Tho: Hall	3	Saml. Glue	2		
Abrah: Tayler	1	Jno. Thomson	3		
Jno. Barnet	1	Danl. Byles	1		
James Longo	1	Tho: Ryding	4		
Tho: Teagle	8	Mary Parrimore	2		
Jno. Cole	5	Tho: Bell, Sr	4		
Jno. Croppier	5	Roger Barker	3		
Robt. Huchinson	6	Giles Cope	3		
Southy Littleton	11				
Hend: Waggaman	1	Mr. Obed: Johnson List			
Edmd. Scarburgh	4	Tho: Parrimore	5		
Wm Stevans	1	Jos: Pittman	2		
Henry Reade	3	James Scamell	1		
Roger Kirkman	1	Nich: Layler	2		
Hugh Yeo	6	George Due	2		
Jno. Frenchman	1	Saml. Atkinson	1		
Danl. Ograyhan	1	Jno. White	1		
		Dorothy Jordain	1		
Mr. Thos: Ryding's List		Tho: Johnson	3		
Tho: Browne	4	Jno. Sheppard	5		
Rich: Sheale	4	James Atkinson	1		
Phill: Fisher	2	Jonas Jackson	--		
Tho: Madux		Jno. Savage	1		

ACCOMACK TITHABLES (Tax Lists): 1663 - 1695

A List of Tithables in Accomack County A. D. 1678

Name	Tithes	Name	Tithes	Name	Tithes
Tho: Parramore	4	Robt. Watson, Sr	5	Mrs. Jordan	2
Rich: Weelch	1	George Smith	1	Rich: Garrison	1
Rhoderick Powell	1	James Camell	1	Obedience Johnson	5
Jno. Sheperd	4	George Roe	1	Jonah Jackson	3
Mrs. Smith	3	Nich: Layler	2	Jno. Gording	2
Edmd. Joyne	2	Robt. Bridge	1	Wm Williams	1
Jno. Lawes	1	Henry Hill	1	Arthur Robins	4
Jno. White	1	George Due	2	Simon Foscue	1
Southy Littleton	9	Jno. Hainering	1	Cornels. Harman	1
Jno. Harmon	1	Tho: Johnson	3	Cornels. Johnson	1
Jno. Roules	1	Joseph Pittman	2	Tho: Marshall	1
Alexandr. Addison	6	Jno. Smith	1	Mr. Tho: Teackle	9
Jno. Booth	2	Jno. Reade	1	Edwd. Ashby	1
Jno. Savidge	2	Francis Robts.	4	Tho: Hall	1
Wm Major	5	Math: Shipp	1	Joseph Clarke	1
Mr. Edwd. Revell	6	Wm Fletcher	2	Dorm: Sulivant	3
Wm Anderson	7	Jno. Smally	1	Robt. Huckson	2
Wm Willson	1	Jno. Washbourne	2	James Atkinson	1
Tho: Williams	1	Ann Charlton	3	Jno. Kellum	1
Rich: Cutler	1	Wm Chace	4	Xopher: Sadbury	1
Garret Supple	1	Jno. Holden	2	Tobias Selby	3
Charles Calvert	1	Geo: Nich: Hack	5	David Gibbins	1
Robt. West	1	George Charnock	2	Tho: Barnet	1
Teage Anderson	3	Jno. Rust	1	Edmd. Scarburgh	6
James Matts	5	Abraham Tayler	1	Robt. Huchinson	7
James Ewel	1	Morgan Thomas	1	Owen Collonon	5
Jno. Barnet	1	Rich: Bally	6	Peter Pritcherd	1
Jno. Nelson	1	Daniel Makerly	1	Jno. Walthom	2
Charles Leatherbury	5	Hendrick Wagaman	1	Roger Mikell	3
Tho: Burrows	1	Jno. Parker, Matapany	10	Mr. Jno. Wise, Sr	9
George Ginn	2	Paul Carter	2	Charles Scarburgh	9
Jno. Parkes	1	Jno. Bishop	2	Robt. Watson	1
Wm Woodhave	1	Stephen Philby	2	George Hope	1
Henry Reade	3	Rich: Piwell	2	Wm Nock	5
Daniel Darby	1	Jno. Fenn	1	Rich: Franklin	1
Wm White	1	Jno. Lewis	1	Tho: Bagwell	2
Edwd Burd	1	And. Stop	1	Tho: Mountford	1
James Longo	2	Jno. Wats, Cooper	3	Jno. Bagwell	1
James Grey	1	Tho: Fowks	3	Edmd. Allen	1
Jno. Macome	1	Wm Silverthorne	1	Robt. Holliday	1
Michol Huet	6	James Fowks	4	Wm Burton	4
Rowld. Savage	3	Jno. Jenkins, Jr	3	Jno. Willis	1
Jno. Lecat	2	Stephn. Warrington	2	Henry Chancy	1
Jno. Milby	1	Robt. Hill	1	Isaack Medcalfe	3
Mrs. Tabitha Brown	13	Tho: Tayler	1	Wm Trasker	2
Rich: Niblet	2	Mr. Hugh Yeo	6	Hen: Williams	2
Rich: Kellum, Sr	7	Jno. Travally	1	James Walker	1
Nich: Tyer	1	Daniel Ogreyhan	1	James Forbus	1
Jno. Fauset	2	Wm Emmot	1	Daniel Owin	1
Edwd. Hitchin	1	Griffith Savage	4	George Johnson	6
Edwd. Smally	1	Jno. Abbot	1	Nich: Millechop	2

21

ACCOMACK TITHABLES (Tax Lists): 1663 - 1695

Name	Tithes	Name	Tithes	Name	Tithes
Samll. Beetch	2	Jno. Mcaell	1	Jno. Blocksum	2
Barth: Meares	4	Jno. Arue	1	Wood: Stokely	2
Jno. Cole	5	Jno. Ares	2	Wm Wallis	2
Arthur Upshot	5	Finlow Mackwilliam	2	Jno. Millson	2
Wm Custis	6	Peter Cleavell	1	Wm Ailworth	3
Nathl. Bradford	10	Wony Macklony	2	Huslin Vanetson	2
Amb: White	7	Roger Ternan	2	Tho: Osburne	6
Jno. Sturgis	2	Tho: Royle	2	Jno. Francisco	2
Peter Parker	3	George Truitt	2	Wm Lowin	2
Wm Martial	2	Rich: Hinman	2	Geo: West	2
Mrs. Fowks	3	Jno. Betts	5	Xopr. Standly	2
Temp: Mason	2	Tho: Nixson	2	Wm Taylor, Jr	4
Rich: Thomson, Sr	2	Tho: Besent	1	Nath: Ratcliff	3
Isack Dix	3	Jno. Tounsend	1	Rich: Hastings	2
Wm White	3	Jno. Barns	4	Jno. Watts, Plantr.	2
Rich: Bundick, Jr	2	Wm German	4	Dennis Morris	2
Rich: Bundick, Sr	3	Wm Onorton	5	Wm Stokely	3
Wm Hickman	1	Christ. Thomson	2	Jno. Ranny	4
Jno. Best	1	Arthur Frame	1	Saml. Tayler	3
Jno. Hanning	1	Timothy Coe	4	Jno. Stokely	3
Wm Parker	3	Jno. Buck	1	Jno. Parsons	2
Edmd. Bowman	11	Majr. Jno. West	12	Peter Walker	2
Tho: Scot	1	Jno. Bowin	4	Jona. Bally	4
Wm Smith	1	Max: Gore	2	Fran: Wharton	2
Daniel Jenifer	26	Robt. Atkinson	1	Ralph Doe	2
Tho: Welburne	4	Edwd. Vahan	1	Jno. Lewis, Sr	4
Wm Taylor, Sr	4	Jonathan Owen	1	Edwd. Brotherton	3
Wm Daniel	2	Jno. Collins	1	George Midleton	4
Wm Brighingham	4	Teage Miskell	1	Jno. Tayler	2
Wm Benston	3	Tho: Smally	1	Walter Tayler	1
Jno. Wallop	10	Tho: Clifton	1	Jno. Drumond	3
Jno. Franklin	2	Wm Kennet	1	Wm Brown	1
Jno. Booth	2	Jno. Chancell	1	Josua Smith	1
Jno. Brookes	4	Bens Canutas	1	Jno. Tarr	1
Jno. Stratton	1	Simn. Smith	1	Danl. Harcard	1
Roger Miles	1	Isack Hester	1	Howil Gladin	1
Jno. Pretiman, Jr	1	Wm Blake	1	Jn Evans	1
Alexdr Massy	1	James Tayler	1	Robt Burton	1
Peter Morgan	1	Coll Littleton, Jen:	3	Robt. Davis	1
Tho: Midleton	1	Morris Dennis	1		

The Total is 694 - v. viii - p.17

A List of Tithables in Accomack county for A.D. 1679

Name	Tithes	Name	Tithes	Name	Tithes
Capt. Daniel Jenifer	24	Oliver Morgen	1	Tho: Smally	1
Mr. Tho: Welburne	5	Jno. Melson	1	Wm Blake, Sr	3
Att Col. Littleton's		Teage Misckell	1	Rich: Hastings	2
Plantacon at Jengotege	5	Will: stokely	2	Wm Kennet	1
Jno. Wallop	7	Christ. Stanly	2	Jno. Stokely	3
Wm Tayler, Sr	6	Jno. Watts, his negro	1	Alex: Massee	2

ACCOMACK TITHABLES (Tax Lists): 1663 - 1695

Name	Tithes	Name	Tithes	Name	Tithes
Wm Tayler, Jr	3	James Tailer	1	Wm Brittingham	6
Woodman Stokly	1	Jno. Brookes	3	Jno. Tarr	1
Daniel Harrard	1	Jno. Booth	3	Tho: Osburne	4
Nath: Ratliff	2	Jno. Franklin	4	Elizab: Bowen	2
Wm Pretteman	1	Simon Smith	1	Peter Walker	3
Joseph Basnet	1	Sebast: Delestase	1	Robt. Atkinson	1
Cuslin Venetson	2	Jno. Evens	1	Jonathan Owen	1
Jno. Stratton	1	Rich: Bundick, Sr	4	Nath: Bradford	9
Edwd Vahan	2	Jno. Hancock	2	Jno. Tankred	1
Tho: Clifton	1	Jno. Jnions	1	Capt. Wm Custis	5
Howel Glading	1	Rich: Bundick, Jr	1	Jno. Arew	1
Jno. Besly	2	Maj. Edmd. Bowman	13	Wm Silverthorne	1
Wm Ailworth	1	Tho: Burrows	1	Wm Jarman	6
Edwd. Thornton	1	Wm White, wheelright	2	Jno. Abbot	2
Wm Lowin	2	Wm Rogers	2	Jno. Carey	1
Geo: West	2	Jno. Jones	3	Joshua Smith	1
Jno. Francisco	2	James Walker	1	Jno. Tounson	1
Wm Benston	3	Tho: Bagwell	2	Robert Davis	1
Robt. Burton	2	Daniel Owen	3	Thomas Bessent	1
Dennis Morris	1	Saml. Beech	2	Fran: Wharton	1
Morris Dennis	3	Mordecay Edwards	1	Roger Miles	1
Jno. Barnes	5	Rich: Franklin	2	Isaack Glover	1
Peter Morgan	1	Arth: Upshot	5	Rodger Ternan	3
Fran: Stokely	1	Geo: Roe	1	Woni Maklanie	4
Tho: Briggs	1	Wm Nock	5	Tho: Rila	--
Jno. Pretiman, Sr	3	Henry Chancey	2	Jno. Ayres	1
Hen: Lurton	1	Jno. Drumond	5	Wm Freeman	1
Jno. Willis	2	Edwd. Brotherton	5	Samuel Tayler	2
Wm Burton	3	Jno. Lewis, Sr	4	Nich: Millechop	3
Hen: Williams	1	Jno. Lawes	1	Wm Daniel	2
Rich: Marriner	1	Wm Onorton	1	Jno. Bloxum	1
Rich: Southern	1	Jno. Parkes	1	Saml. Sandford	1
Isaack Medcalfe	1	Griffith Savadge	3	Tho: Barnes	1
Edmd. Allen	2	Rich: Hinman	2	Hum: Toft	1
Tho: Nickson	2	Wm Martiall	2	Edwd. Hichin	1
Robt. Watson	1	Peter Parker	2	Rich: Paritson	1
Arthur Frame	1	Wm Parker	2	Jno. Bagwell	3
Wm Davis	1	Wm Brown	1	Joseph Brown	4
Jno. Hornsby	1	Jno. Hanning	1	Barth: Meares	4
Jno. Bets	3	Jno. Sturges	2	Joseph Thorne	1
George Midleton	4	Geo: Hope	4	Wm Trafford	1
Rich: Johnson	2	Isaac Dix	4	Jno. Cole	7
Finlow Mackwilliam	1	Tho: Evans	2	Simond Forme	1
Capt. Rich: Hill	4	James Fowkes	3	Cornelius Harman	1
Xopher Thomson	1	Steph: Filby	1	Wm Williams	1
Ralph Doe	2	Jno. Travally	1	Edm: Joyne	1
Jno. Parker	10	Wm Sill	1	Fran: Roberts	4
Jno. Matts	5	Jno. White	1	Jno. Hamering	2
Majr. Cha: Scarburgh	5	Coll Sou: Littleton	8	Joseph Newton	3
Nich: Layler	1	Capt. Hill: Stringer	13	Lewis Johnson	3
George Due	2	Saml. Serjent	2	Danl. Darby	1
Charles Leatherbury	2	Tho: Tayler	1	Hen: Hill	1
Jno. Nelson	1	Jno. Tayler	5	Samson Doss	1

ACCOMACK TITHABLES (Tax Lists): 1663 - 1695

Name	Tithes	Name	Tithes	Name	Tithes
Jno. Kellam	2	Tho: Scott	4	Alexandr. Addyson	5
Jno. Clark	1	Lieut. Coll. West	11	Widdow Jackson	2
Tho: Morgin	1	Mr. Jno. Wise	9	Arthur Robins	5
Jno. Mecome	1	Tho: Fowkes	2	Xopher Sadbury	1
Jno. Rowles	2	Jno. Watts	2	Jno. Booth	3
Edwd. Burd	1	Paul Carter	1	Tho: Parramore	4
David Gibons	1	Rich: Piwell	2	Rich: Meltin	1
Jno. Smally	1	Rich: Cutler	1	James Camell	1
James Gray	1	Phill: Quinton	1	Tho: Marshall, Sr.	2
Wm Fletcher	2	Charles Calvert	1	Jno. Smith	1
Denis Silleivent	1	James Ewell	1	Jno. Reade	1
Capt. Edmd. Scarburgh	6	James Bonewell	2	Geo: Anthony	1
Jno. Lecatt	3	Jno. Fenn	2	Tho: Johnson	3
Jno. Milby	1	Jno. Lewis	1	Jona. Johnson	1
Rich: Neblet	2	Andrew Stop	1	Obe: Johnson	5
Wm Major	4	Tho: Hedge	1	Robt. Watson	4
Geo: Walthom	2	Edwd. Revell	3	Wm Williams	1
Geo: Ginn	3	Wm Cleverdon	4	Jno. Savage	2
Rowland Savage	4	Daniel Ograhan	1	Widow Jordan	2
Wm Turner	1	Jno. Jenkins, Jr.	2	Wm Goulding	1
Hen: Read	4	Stephen Warrington	2	Roger Berker	2
Nich: Tyler	1	Wm Anderson	8	Jno. Sheperd	3
Rich: Kellum	5	Peter Pritchett	2	Geo: Smith	4
Geo: Charnock	1	Teage Anderson	2	Garret Sipple	1
Jno. Howding	1	Hen: Selman	1	William Chace	4
George Russell	3	Wm White	1	Daniel Makarty	1
Jno. Barnes	1	James Longo	1	Rich: Bally	7
Abraham Tayler	1	Tho: Hall	1	Jno. Washbourne	3
Geo: Nich: Hack	8	Peter Yorke	2	Hend: Wagaman	1
Jacob Morris	1	Mr. Teakle	6	Robt. Huchinson	6
Robt. Watson, Jr.	2	Tob: Selby	5	Dormt. Sullivant	3
Robt. Hudson	1	Owen Collonon	4	Joseph Clark	1
Jno. Parkes	1	Jno. Browton	1	Mikol Hewet	7

Ye Total is 683
5 more Tithables omitted to be added 5
688   - v. viii - p. 99

A List of Tithables in Accomack County A. D. 1680

Name	Tithes	Name	Tithes	Name	Tithes
Tho: Welburne	4	Isaac Dix	6	Wm Willson	1
Max: Gore	2	Tho: Dent	1	Henry Allen	1
Jno. Wallop	7	Edmd. Joynes	1	Henry Chancy	2
Jno. Drumond	4	Rich: Hinman	2	Jno. Jones	3
Arthur Upshur	7	Hen: Williams	2	Wm Willet, Const:	3
Robt. Hill	1	Coll Jno. Custin	7	Wm Major	3
Xophr. Stanly	1	Jno. Abbot	2	Griffin Savage	1
Jno. Booth, Pocomk.	3	Wm Wyat	1	Edward Mills	1
Phill: Quinton	1	Samuel Sandford	3	Jno. Stretton	1
James Walker	1	James Tayler	1	Wood: Stokley	1
Wm Lowin	2	Wm Burton	5	Joseph Stokley	1

ACCOMACK TITHABLES (Tax Lists): 1663 - 1695

Name	Tithes	Name	Tithes	Name	Tithes
Nicholas Millechop	3	Robt. Holliday	1	Wm Prettiman, Jr.	1
Daniel Harwood	1	Daniel Owin	2	Rich: Cutler	1
Wm Fletcher	2	Richard Hasting	2	Dennis Morris	2
Peter Clevill	1	Wm Nock	5	Joshua Lee	1
Howel Glading	1	Thomas Glew	1	Jno. Smally	1
Jno. Francisco	3	Nicholas Layler	1	Wm Freeman	1
Wm Kennet	1	Edward Moore, Sr.	1	Jno. Brookes	4
Wm Stokley	2	Jno. Hammering	1	Wm Wreathwell	1
Wm Wright	1	Hen: Hill	1	Abraham Tayler	2
Edwd. Vahan	2	Thomas Fookes	1	Geo: Hope	5
Wm German	6	Xophr: Calvert	1	Arthur Frame	1
Jno. Johnson	1	Nathl. Ratcliff	2	Jno. Willis, Sr.	2
James Scamell	1	Morris Dennis	3	Robt. Burton	1
Jno. Hamering	1	Jno. Lewis, Sr.	3	Samuel Tayler	2
Geo: Dewy	2	Robt. Atkins	1	Jno. Barnes	3
Thom: Parramore	4	Jno. Tankred	1	Joseph Besnet	1
Jno. White	1	Jno. Prettiman, Sr.	1	Robt. Hudson	1
Jno. Thomson	3	Tho: Besant	1	Jno. Bagwell	4
Wm Lingo	1	Tho: Smally	1	Hen: Sellman	1
Richd. Melson	1	Teige Miskell	1	Richd. Garritson	1
Rich: Franklin	1	Wm Turner	1	Garret Supple	1
Daniel Darby	2	Samuel Beech	2	James Conners	1
Jno. Washbourne	3	Geo: West	3	Thomas Allen	1
David Gibbons	1	James Foster	1	Jno. Walthom	4
Richd. Niblet	1	Richard Richards	1	Jno. Wheeler	1
Thoms. Hall	1	Jno. Read	1	Tho: Bagwell	2
Francis Stokley	1	Jno. Evans	1	Geo: Parker, Jr.	2
Samuel Cob	2	Jno. Jenkins, Jr.	3	Peter Morgan	1
Jonathan Owen	2	James Fookes	3	Richard Johnson, Jr	2
Alexander Addison	2	Edward Revell	3	Jno. Cole	5
Roger Mikell	4	Wm Chace	3	Wm Bunton	2
Dormt. Sullivant	4	Jno. Savage	1	Jno. Nellson	1
Jno. Smith	1	Edmd. Scarburgh	4	Isaac Metcalfe	4
Wm Williams	1	Tho: Buchell	1	Jno. Parker, tayler	2
Wony Macklany	3	Jno. Parke	1	Wm Custis	6
Geo: Nich: Hack	5	Geo: Ginn	1	Wm Daniel	2
Richd. Bundick, Jr.	2	Tho: Willson	1	Jno. Best	1
Jno. Hancock	1	Jno. Broton	1	Roger Barker	2
Daniel Makarty	1	Joseph Brown	3	Dorothy Jordan	2
Xopher Sadbury	1	Jno. Frankling	2	Jno. Macom	1
Edward Hitchen	1	Jno. Rowles	4	Robt. Dunbar	2
Robt. Watson, Jr.	1	Jno. Thomson	1	Jno. Wise, Sr.	9
James Longo	2	Jno. Clarke	2	Teige Anderson	3
Wm Ailworth	1	Jno. Fisher	2	Wm White	4
Edward Thornton	1	Jno. Barker	1	Jno. Onions	1
Jno. Best	1	Nathanl. Bradford	9	Jno. Tounsend	1
Jno. Lawes	1	Francis Wharton	1	Jno. Blocksom	1
Jno. Clarke	1	Thoms. Nixson	2	Jno. Parker, Sr.	7
Cha: Letherbury	2	Wm Parker	3	Tho: Clark	1
Tho: Osburn	3	Jno. Barnet	1	Robt. Watson	5
Rowland Savage	5	Morgin Thomas	2	Clement Only	1
Thomas Marshall	2	Hendrick Wagaman	1	Jno. Booth	3
Richd. Bundick, Sr.	2	Baptist Newcom	1	Geo: Truit	1
Ralph Doe	2	Barthol: Meers	3	Francis Roberts	4

ACCOMACK TITHABLES (Tax Lists): 1663 - 1695

	Tithes		Tithes		Tithes
James Matts	5	Robt. Watson	1	Nicholas Tyler	1
Jno. Barke	1	Jno. Hanning	1	Wm Tayler, Jr.	4
Tho: Scudamore	1	Jno. Kellum	3	Stephen Warrington	3
Jno. Collins	1	Wm Tayler, Sr.	9	Jno. Shepherd	4
Nich: Dun	1	Nickolas Newman	3	Wm Benston	3
Peter Walker	3	Jno. Milby	1	Cants. Bence	1
Samson Doe	1	Tho: Johnson	3	Jno. Melson	2
Richd. Johnson	1	Jno. Aires	3	Henry Read	6
Tho: Reyly	2	Joseph Newton	2	Thomas Smally	1
Jno. Carey	1	Henry Toules	3	Robt. Hutchinson	4
Wm Anderson	10	Widdow Hewet	5	Jno. Lecat	3
Jno. Watts, Cooper	2	Edmd. Bowman	10	Arthur Robins	4
Tho: Tayler	1	Jno. West	17	Peter Watkinson	1
Francis Benson	1	Peter Parker	2	James Gray	1
Wm Browne	1	Wm Blake	2	Richd. Hill	5
Wm Brittingham	5	Thoms. Webb	2	Gueslin Venetson	2
Obed: Johnson	4	Daniel Jenifer	26	Symon Foskew	1
Hillary Stringer	3	Alexander Massy	--	Cornelus Harman	1
Geo: Smith	6	Wm Osburn	1	Tobias Selby	4
Wm Betty	1	Jno. Stokley	2	Peter Parker	1
Edwd. Kellum	1	Dennis Sullivant	1	Att Coll Little-	
Richd. Bayley	5	Peter Pritchet	1	ton's Planta.	8
Wm White	1	Paul Carter	2	Saml. Serjent	1
Stephen Philbe	1	Cha: Scarburgh	7	Thomas Lucas	1
Jno. Lewis	1	Wm Fleare	1	Andrew Stop	1
Wm Martiall	2	Richard Piwell	1	George Johnson	5
Edward Brotherton	2	Wm Onorton	1	Widdow Jackson	3
Wm Hickman	1	Jno. Watts, Planter	3	Xopher Thomson	1
Richard Kellum	4	Jno. Holding	1	Jno. Sturges	3
Sebast Delastacios	1	Roger Miles	2	Roger Ternon	3
Wm Cleverdon	4	Timothy Coe	3	Daniel Ograhan	1
Joseph Clark	1	Oliver Morgan	1	Jno. Fenn	1
Geo: Charnock	1	Hen: Lurton	1	Alex: Massey	2
Owen Collonon	6	Since Added			
Wm Silverthorne	1	James Ewell	1	Wm Brown	1
Wm Sill & Joseph)		Wm Davis	1	Mr. Teakle	3
Robinson)	2	Otho Prophet	2	Abrah: Tayler, Jr	1
Majr Scarburgh 2)		Wm Brown	1	Francis Benston	1
negroes omitted)	2	Anth: West	1	Wm Bradford	1
Mrs. Mary Scarburgh 1)		Tho: Dangerfield,)			
negro called Tongo)	1	liveing with Mr)	1		
		Sandford)			

Total 700 - v. vi - p. 211

A List of Tithables in Accomack County A.D. 1681

Paul Tanner	1	Wm Lowin	2	Danl. Jenifer	24
John Evans	1	Jno. Clark	2	Geo: Midleton	2
John Beasly	1	Edward Thornton	1	Jno. Arew	1
Oliver Morgan	1	Jno. Collins	1	Wm Onoughton	1

ACCOMACK TITHABLES (Tax Lists): 1663 - 1695

	Tithes		Tithes		Tithes
John Booth	2	Wm Stokeley	2	Wm Leitchfeild	1
John Franklin	2	George West	4	Geo: Trewit	1
John Watts, Constble.	2	Jno. Millington	1	Josh: Smith	1
Van Netson	2	James Tayler	1	Tho: Blake	2
Tho: Osburne	4	James Booth	1	Wm Silverthorne	1
Wm Tayler, Jr.	4	Cants. Bens	1	Wm Bunting	2
Maxa: Gore	3	Peter Clavill	1	Wm Brittingham	6
Sebast. Delastatius	1	Saml. Oliver	1	Wm Benston	1
Teage Miscall	1	Tho: Nixcon	2	John Brookes	4
John Blades	1	Tho: Besant	1	Wood: Stokely	1
Amos Cooke	1	Jno. Townsend	1	Tho: Welburne	4
Tho: Prophet	1	Jno. Deane	1	Wm Aylworth	1
Roger Miles	1	Jno. Carey	1	Wm Tayler, Sr.	7
Jno. Blocksum	1	Jno. Littleton	1	Francis Wharton	3
Joseph Basnet	1	Rich: Johnson	1	Wm Wyatt	1
Wm Kenet	1	Rich: Johnson, Jr.	1	Alexandr. Massy	1
Jno. Mellson	1	Wm Johnson	1	Morris Dennis, Sr	2
Peter Parker	1	Dennis Morris	2	Ben: Eyre	2
Howel Glading	1	Richd. Hinman	1	Jno. Stokeley	2
Roger Ternan	2	Robt. Halle	1	Alexandr. Dun	1
Wony Macklany	2	Peter Walker	2	Nath: Ratcliff	2
Jno. Drumond	5	Wm Daniel	2	Jno. Barker	1
Jno. Parker	2	Tho: Townsend	1	Jno. Francisco	1
Geo: Wheeler	8	Jno. Stratton	2	Fran: Hutchinson	2
John Abbot	2	Joseph Stokely	2	Jno. Prittiman	1
Jno. Lewis, Sr.	3	Rich: Hasting	1	Wm Prettiman	1
Tho: Rilack	1	Peter Morgan	2	Robt Watson, Sr.	1
Chr. Thomson	1	Wm Morgan	1	Robt. Atkinson	1
Arthur Frame	1	Robt. Davis	1	Wm Freeman	1
Edw: Brotherton	1	Robert Burton	2	Henry Towles	2
Jno. Bally	6	Tho: Briggs	1	Jno. Wallop	9
Joseph Brickill	3	Wm Hickman	1	Wm Cleverdon	4
George Hope	3	Rich: Cutler	1	Barth: Meares	5
Jno. Barnes	2	Jno. Barker	1	Isack Metcalf	4
Walter Harges	1	Rich: Bundick	2	Tho: Tayler	1
Hen: Williams	2	Wm White	3	Jno. Watts	1
Saml. Beech	2	Rich: Numan	1	Jno. Tutchberry	1
Jno. Bagwell	2	Robt. Gillrean	1	Joseph Newton	4
Jno. Hancock	1	Danl. Ograyan	2	Wm Burton	5
Geo: Parker	2	Peter Pritchard	1	Nath: Bradford	10
Jno. Sturgis	4	Wm Mason	1	Jno. Tankred	2
Jno. Wheeler	2	James Wathen	1	Hen: Hill	1
Isaack Dix	4	Hen: Lurton	1	Hen: Chancey	2
Wm Marshall	3	Cha: Calvert	2	Wm Custis	4
Jno. Onions	1	Edwd. Revell	5	Edwd. Kellum	1
Robt. Edge	1	Jno. Jenkins	4	Tho: Parramore	2
Edmd. Bowman	13	Jno. Wise	9	Tho: Marshall	2
Peter Parker	4	Tho: Webb	2	Roger Barker	2
Wm Parker	3	Jno. West	14	Jno. Reade	1
Wm Browne	1	Tege Andros	3	Jno. Smith	1
Daniel Jones	1	Phillip Quinton	1	Tho: Glew	1
Jno. Simcock	1	James Ewell	1	James Camell	1
Jno. Hanning	2	Tho: Fookes	2	Jno. Thomson	3
Hum: Trught	1	Jno. Michaell	4	Tho: Johnson	2

ACCOMACK TITHABLES (Tax Lists): 1663 - 1695

Name	Tithes	Name	Tithes	Name	Tithes
Cha: Scarburgh	8	Arthur Donis	1	Jno. Johnson	1
Jno. Parker	6	Jno. Cole	5	Jno. White	1
Jno. Fenn	1	Tho: Bagwell	4	Nicholas Laylar	1
Rich: Pywell	1	Arthur Upshott	7	Jno. Hammering	1
Stephen Fillby	1	Daniel Owen	2	Xopr. Sadbury	1
Andrew Stop	1	Jno. Willis, Sr.	2	Jno. Fisher	1
Jno. Lewis	2	Edwd. Hichin	1	Jno. Savage	1
Tho: Allen	1	Wm Williams	1	Stephen Warrington	2
Rich: Garrittson	1	Cornelius Johnson	1	James Bonwell	1
Wm Nock	4	Jno. Lawes	1	Wm Anderson	10
Jno. Jones	1	Geo: Smith	5	Robert Hill	1
Wm Thoroton	1	Ralph Doe, Sr.	3	James Fooks	2
Edwd. Burd	1	Jno. Clarke	2	Mrs. Jackson	2
Jno. Mecom	1	Att Coll Littleton's	6	Tho: Palmer	1
Geo: Hack	7	Richd. Jones	3	Tho: Dent	1
Robt. Hudson	1	Richard Bally	5	Jno. Scot	1
Tho: Teakle	4	James Davis	3	Arthur Robins	4
Wm Fletcher	3	Rich: Richards	1	Edmd. Joyne	1
George Charnock	2	Geo: Johnson, Sr.	)	Jno. Cobb	2
Jno. Holden	2	Geo: Johnson, Jr.	)	Alexandr. Addison	3
Wm Major	3	Wm Foster	) 5	Jno. Booth	4
Dormt. Sullivant	2	Simon Tege	)	Robt. Watson, Sr.	5
James Gray	1	Tho: Teage	)	Jno. Wouldhave	1
Edmd. Scarburgh	4	Coll West 1 more	1	Obed: Johnson	3
Owen Collonon	4	Mrs. Matts	4	Francis Roberts	4
Wm White	2	Tim: Coe	3	Robt. Hutchinson	5
Tobias Selvy	4	Capt. Custis for Tho:		Rich: Jones, Sr.	4
Jno. Parke	2	Chambers	1	Saml. Serjent	1
Joshua Lee	1	Capt. Hill	1	Clemt. Onely	1
Nich: Dun	1	John Shepherd	3	Wm Chace	3
Jacob Morris	1	Tongo at Mrs Scar-		Geo: Russell	2
Henry Selman	1	burghs	1	Mr. Sandford	4
Morgan Thomas	1	Wm Blake	3	Jno. Lecat	1
Jno. Nelson	1	Nich: Millechop	1	James Longo	2
Tho: Hall	1	2 negroes on Coll)		Rich: Kellum, Sr.	4
Hen: Read	5	Littleton: Land)	2	Jno. Fox	1
Jno. Smally	1	Tho: Scott		Robt. Dunbar	1
Hercules Shepherd	2	Rowland Savage	3	Daniel Darby	2
Jno. Kellam	2	Peter Watkinson	1	Hillary Stringer	3
Hend: Wagaman	1	Jno. Milby	2	Jno. Barnet	1
Rich: Niblet	2	Abraham Tayler	3	Tho: Jenkins	1
Jno. Breton	1	Jno. Rowles	1	John Melson	1
Jno. Washbourne	2	Wm Simons	1	Geo: Ginn	1
Jno. Walthom	3	Tho: Wilson	1	Nich: Tiler	1
Wm Abchurch	1				

Total 677 -v. vi - p. 283

A List of Tithables in Accomack County of ye yeare 1682

Name	Tithes	Name	Tithes	Name	Tithes
Capt. Walops List		Kanutus Bence	1	Tho: Welburne	5
Roburt Atkins	1	John Hancock	1	Samuel Tayler	2
John Wallop	5	John Evans	2	Jno. Francisco	3

ACCOMACK TITHABLES (Tax Lists): 1663 - 1695

Name	Tithes	Name	Tithes	Name	Tithes
Richd. Hastings	1	Sebest. Delastatius	1	Edmd. Allen	1
Edwd. Thornton	1	Roger Miles	1	Hen: Allen, Jr.	1
Henry Toules	1	Danl. Harwood	1	Isaac Metcalfe	3
Joseph Bassnet	1	John Tounsend	1	Edwd. Burd	1
Wm Blake	3	John Bloxum	1	Jno. Terry	1
Wm Aleworth	1	Wm Morgan	1	Saml. Beech	1
Symon Smith	1	Wm Jones	1	Hen: Chancy	1
John Beasly	1	Nathl. Ratcliff	2	Wm Custis	3
Wm Anderson	7	Robt. Davis	2	Nathl. Bradford	9
John Stockeley	1	Ben: Eyre	2	Hen: Hill	1
Joseph Stockeley	2			Hen: Lurton	1
Jno. Watts	2	Majr. Bowman's List			
Francis Stokely	1	John Bagwell	4	Capt. Hill's List	
Wm Daniel	2	John Jones	1	John Drumond	3
John Prettiman	2	Peter Parker	3	Timothy Coe	2
Alexandr. Massey	1	Wm Brown, Sr.	1	Geo: Johnson	4
James Tayler	1	John Williams	1	Geo: Truet	2
Wm Benston	2	Isaac Dix	4	Tho: Nixson	3
Richd. Floues	1	John Wheeler	1	John Wilson	1
Barnet Ramsy	1	John Barnes	2	Jno. Deane	1
Wm Whright	1	Tho: Burrows	1	Nich: Newman	1
Hen: Sadberry	1	David Jones	1	Xophr. Thomson	1
Van: Nettson	1	Jno. Sturgis	3	Tho: Blake	2
Howel Glading	2	Geo: Hope	2	Jno. Carie	1
Morris Dennis	1	John Hanning	1	Finla Mackwilliam	1
Dennis Morris	2	Geo: Parker	2	Arthur Frame	1
Wm Brittingham	4	Richd. Therrit	1	Wm Bunting	1
Max: Gore	3	Wm Parker	2	Wm Willet	1
Jno. Melson	1	Richd. Bundick	2	Geo: Midleton	1
John Brooks	2	Richd. Johnson	1	Wm Silverthorne	2
Edwd. Moore	2	Wm Marshall	1	John Abbot	1
Saml. Sandford	5	Wm White	3	Peter Clavell	1
Wood: Stockeley	2	Jno. Onions	2	John Arew	1
Wm Tayler, Jr.	4	Wm Hickman	1	Rich: Hinman	1
Teage Miskell	1	Edmd. Bowman	9	Wonie Macklanne	2
Tho: Briggs	2	Wm Brown, Jr.	1	Roger Ternan	1
Ralf Justice	2	Wm Burton	6	Tho: Ryla	1
Robert Burton	1	Francis Wharton	1	Jno. Lewis, Jr.	1
Daniel Jenifer	21			Joshua Smith	1
Robt. Watson	1	Capt. Custis List		Jno. Lewis, Sr.	3
Giles Monfreson	1	Hen: Williams	3	Wm Onorton	1
Richd. Hinman	2	Tho: Bagwell	4	James Trewit	1
Geo: West	3	John Willis, Sr.	2	Wm Leitchfield	1
Richd. Hill	2	Richd. Garrittson	1	John Baylie	6
John Barrick	1	Edwd. Hichin	1	Richd. Hill	3
John Stratton	1	Tho: Allum	1		
Edwd. Vahan	1	Edwd. Kellam	1	Majr. Scarburgh's List	
Wm Jerman	4	Tho: Tayler	1	Cha: Scarburgh	10
Wm Tayler, Sr.	6	Hen: Custis	1	Jno. Fenn	2
Tho: Prossit	1	Wm Nock	4	Jno. Lewis	1
Jno. Franklin	3	Barth: Meares	4	Andrew Stop	1
Wm Stockely	2	Arthur Upshot	8	Richd. Piwell	1
Peter Walker	3	Jno. Michaell	4	Jno. Watts, Cooper	2
Wm Wayle	1	John Cole	5		

ACCOMACK TITHABLES (Tax Lists): 1663 - 1695

	Tithes		Tithes		Tithes
Joseph Newton	2	James Davis	4	Ralph Doe	2
Teage Andros	3	John Waltom	4	Richard Owen	1
Phillip Quinton	1	John Spiars	1	Coll: West	16
Richd. Cutler	1	John Rowles	3	Tho: Scot	1
Jno. Kellam	1	Wm Chace	2	Jno. Cobb, Constble	2
James Tissaker	1	Jonathan Newton	1	Capt Edm: Scarburgh	5
Tho: Evans	1	Arnold Harrison	3	Tho: Webb	-
James Bonwell	1	Tho: Teackle	3	Robt. Halle	1
Jno. Jenkins	4	Jno. Lecatt	2	Jno. Barker	-
Stephen Warrington	3	Wm Major	2	Jno. Millington	1
John Lawes	2	Richd. Jones, Sr.	3	Jno. Parker, Tayler	-
Tho: Fooks	2	Richd. Hoveington	1	Wm Thoroton	1
Cha: Leatherbury	2	Hen: Selman	1	Edwd. Brotherton	2
Jno. Wise	8	James Longo	1	Doctr. Dewy	1
Jno. Tutchberry	1	Richd. Melton	1	Walter Harges	1
Jno. Charles	5	Richd. Jones, Jr.	2	James Wathan	1
Danl. Ograhon	2	Abraham Tayler	2	Robt. Edge	1
Jno. Parker	6	Jno. Smally	2	Fran: Bateson	1
James Fookes	2	Tho: Hall	1	Doctr. Jenkins	2
Peter Pritchet	1	Richd. Bally	4	Nich: Millechop	2
Jno. Stanton	1	John Barnet	1	Wm Mason	1
Flor: Matts	4	Geo: Nich: Hack	7	Wm Wise, Jr.	1
Edwd. Revell	4	Nathl. Tunnill	1		
		Francis Roberts	4	Total 628	
Mr. Bally's List		John Clark	1		
Jno. Washbourne	2	Arthur Robins	7	v. vi - p. 315	
Jno. Nelson	1	Robt. Watson, Sr.	5		
Dormt. Sullivant	2	Robt. Watson, Jr.	2		
Hen: Read	5	Dorothy Jordan	2		
Rowl: Savage	3	Wm Williams	1		
Tho: Bushell	7	Simon Foskew	1		
Nich: Dunn	1	Cornelius Harman	2		
Saml. Serjent	1	Edmd. Joyne	1		
Clemt. Only	1	Lydia Jackson	2		
Geo: Charnock	2	Tho: Parramore	4		
Tho: Willson	1	Geo: Smith	3		
John Broton	2	Tho: Johnson	3		
John Holden	2	Tho: Lucus	1		
John Parkes	1	Alex: Addison	2		
Wm Fletcher	3	Nich: Laylor	1		
Owen Collonon	4	John White	1		
Robt. Hutchinson	3	Jno. Johnson	1		
John Milby	2	James Camell	1		
Geo: Ginn	1	Tho: Clarke	1		
Richd. Niblet	1	Jos: Clarke	1		
John Macom	1	Christo: Sadbury	1		
James Gray	2	Tho: Marshall	2		
Peter Watkinson	1	Roger Barker	2		
Danl. Darby	1	Thomas Glue	1		
Nicho: Tyler	1	Obed: Johnson	3		
Richd. Wood	1	John Shepherd	3		
Richd. Kellum	4	John Smith	1		
Wm Milby	3	John Read	2		
Wm White	2	John Hamering	2		

30

ACCOMACK TITHABLES (Tax Lists): 1663 - 1695

The List of Tithables in Accomack County for ye year 1683

Name	Tithes	Name	Tithes	Name	Tithes
Mr. Tho: Welburne's List		Wm Jones	1	Isaac Medcalfe	1
Tho: Prophet	3	Teage Miskell	1	Wm Daniel	2
Wm Aileworth	1	John Stratton	2	Hen: Williams	2
Edwd. Thorneton	1	Nath: Ratcliffe	3	Jno. Wouldhave	1
Ben: Eyres	3	Saml. Tayler	3	Tho: Bagwell	3
Tob: Bull	1	Jno. Prettiman	1	Jno. Bagwell	3
Richd. Hastings	1	Jno. Prettiman, Jr.	1	Wm Burton	5
Max: Gore	3	Hen: Allin	1	Jno. How	2
Peter Walker	1	Oliver Morgan	1	Saml. Beech	1
Wm Whright	1	Christ: Morgan	1	Jno. Clarke	2
N. Mellson	1	Simon Smith	1	Wm Nock	3
John Watts	2	Edwd. Moore	1	Ed: Hitchin	1
Jno. Wilkinson	1	John Jackson	1	Hen: Chancey	1
John Evans	1	Wood: Stockley	1	Walt: Harges	3
Amos Cooke	1	Richd. Craige	1	Jno. Cole	3
Kants. Bents	1	James Armstrong	1	Art: Upshot	5
Tho: Thomas	1	John Hancock	1	Nath: Bradford	8
Saml. Sandford	3	Wm Tayler, Sr.	6	Edwd. Burd	1
Hen: Tolls	2	Wm Tayler, Jr.	3	Jno. Terrey	1
Jonath. Owen	3	Wm Stockly	2	Robt Edge	1
Jos: Stockley	1	Hen: Bromevill	1	Wm Custis	3
Fran: Stockly	1	Wm Atkins	1		
Fran: Stockly	1			Capt. Johnson's	
Nath: Tunnell	2	Majr. Bowman's precints.		prects.	
Wm Blake	2	Wm Brown	1	Obed: Johnson	4
Wm Blake, Jr.	2	Wm Parker	2	Simon Foscew	1
Jno. Francisco	1	John Hanning	1	Corn: Harman	1
Hen: Sadbury	1	John Sturges	2	Arth: Gall	1
James Tayler	1	Geo: Parker	2	Wm Betts	1
Bernard Ramsy	1	John Barnes	2	Wm Williams	1
Wm Brittenham	5	Tho: Burrows	1	Edmd. Joynes	1
Wm Daniel	2	John Wheeler	1	Tho: Tayler	1
Alex: Massy	1	Tho: Cripping	5	Geo: Smith	4
Rich: Flowers	1	Geo: Hope	5	Robt. Watson	5
Wm Benston	2	Peter Parker	1	Tho: Clarke	1
Ed: Felton	1	Rich: Johnson	1	Joseph Clarke	1
Wm Wyat	1	Wm Marshall	1	Fran: Robins	4
Robt. Atkinson	1	John Jnions	2	Rich: Garritson	2
John Collins	1	Hen: Hubanck	1	Ed: Kellam	1
Wm Anderson	13	Edwd. Gelson	1	Tho: Lucas	1
Tho: Welburne	3	Gertrud Cropper		Tho: Parramore,	
Jno. Deane	1	Tithbles.	2	Constble	2
Robt. Farrington	3	Edmd. Bowman	7	James Camell	1
Daniel Harwood	1	Isaac Dix	4	Tho: Johnson	2
Howel Glading	2	Rich: Bundick	2	Sara White, Wid:	1
John Booth	1			Ralph Doe	2
Daniel Jenifer	19	Capt. Custis prcincts.		John Hamering	1
Geo: West	2	Jno. Willis, Sr.	2	Geo: Anthony	1
John Beasly	1	Hen: Custis	2	Jno. Fisher	1
Nich: Millechop	3	Widow Meers	3	Jno. Shepherd	3
Jno. Franklin	4	John Michaell	2	Geo: Dewy	2
Sebast: Delastatius	1	James Walker	2	Lyd: Jackson	3

ACCOMACK TITHABLES (Tax Lists): 1663 - 1695

Name	Tithes	Name	Tithes	Name	Tithes
John Savage	1	Richd. Jones, Sr.	2	Widow Cleverdon's Tithbles.	5
Dor: Jordan	1	Rich: Jones, Jr.	2	Wm Thoroton	2
Tho: Marshall	3	Jona: Newton	2	John Lewis	1
Roger Barker	1	Jno. Waker	1	Andrew Stop	1
John Smith	1	Richd. Kellam	3	Phill: Quinton	2
John Reade	1	Saml. Serjent	1	Tho: Fooks	3
John Scamell	1	Clemt. Only	1	John Parker,Tayler	1
Arth: Robins	6	James Davis	1	Stephen Filby	1
		Arnold Harrison	2	Steven Warrington	3
Mr Bally's prcints.		Widow Hall's Tithbls.	1	James Foster	2
Mr. Tho: Teackle	3	Dormt. Sullivant	2	Rich: Pywell	1
John Walthom	3	Abraham Tayler	2	John Jenkins, Sr.	5
Jno. Simcock	3	Richd. Bally	5	James Tissaker	1
Jno. Spires	1	Geo: Nich: Hack	6	Fran: Batson	3
Geo: Ginn	1			Wm Phillips	1
Jno. Chandler	1	Capt. Hill's prcints		John Watts,Cooper	1
Jno. Chace	1	Jno. Baily	7	Tho: Bernet	1
Own. Collonon	5	Geo: Johnson	2	John Michison	1
Wm Fletcher	4	Dennis Morris	2	James Nathan	1
Jno. Smally	1	Wm Rust	1	John Lawes	2
Edmd. Scarburgh	4	Tho: Blake	3	Teage Andrson	3
Tho: Bushell	5	John Carey	1	Wm Mason	1
Jn Rowles	3	Robt Davis	2	Rich: Cutler	1
Hen: Selman	1	John Trewit	1	John Kellam	2
Jno. Holden	2	Tho: Nickson	1	John Parker, Sr.	6
Geo: Charnock	1	Fran: Wharton	1	Cha: Leatherbury	3
Wm Chace	2	Morris Dennis	2	James Fowks	2
Wm Pilcher	1	Arthur Frame	1	James Bonwell	1
John Sparkes	2	Tho: Rilla	1	Peter Pritchet	3
Jno. Milby	1	Jno. Lewis	4	Cha: Scarburgh	10
James Longo	1	Roger Ternan	1	Mrs. Mats Tithbls	5
Rich: Wood	1	Wm Bunting	1	Edwd. Revell	4
Jno. Washbourne	2	Wony Macklanie	2	Danl. Ograhan	2
Robt. Hutchinson	3	Wm Jerman	4	John Wise, Sr.	7
Hen: Read	4	John Drumond	3	Wm Sill	1
John Barnet	2	Wm Dennison	1	Wm Wise	1
Rich: Hoveington	1	John Arew	1	Jno. West	16
Tho: Willson	2	James Truitt	1	Wm Lowing	1
John Broughton	2	Finlaw Mackwilliam	1	John Townsend	1
Rich: Niblet	1	Wm Leitchfield	1	Wm West	1
Wm White	2	Geo: Midleton	1	Robt. Burton	1
John Lecatt	2	Wm Silverthorne	2	Richard Hinman	3
Danl Darby	1	Joshua Smith	1	Robt. Hawly	1
Hen: Hall	1	Tho: Webb	2	Jno. Hudson	1
Jno. Mellony	1	Christ: Thomson	1	Robt. Lambert	1
Peter Watkinson	2	Nich: Newman	1	Jno. Blockson	1
Nich: Dunn	1	John Abbot	2	Jno. Barnick	1
Joseph Amos	2	Geo: Truit	1	Ralph Justice	1
Richd. Melton	1	Tho: Scot	2	Rich: Greenal	1
Wm Milby	3	Edwdl. Brotherton	3	Timothy Coe	2
Wm Major	2			Henry Lurton	1
Rich: Powell	1	Tithbles. in Maj. Chas: Scarburgh's precincts			
John Nelson	1				
Rowld. Savage	4	John Fenn	1	v. vi - p. 356	

ACCOMACK TITHABLES (Tax Lists): 1663 - 1695

The List of Tithbles. in Accomack County for ye yeare 1684

	Tithes		Tithes		Tithes
Mr. Welburne and Capt		Ben: Eyre	2	Arthur Upshot	8
Wallop's Presincts		John Hancock	1	Hen: Williams	2
John Wallop	5	Jno. Bloxum	1	James Walker	3
At Dor: Watts)		Nich: Millechop	2	Hen: Custis	2
Tho: Wooslee)		Wm Brittenham	6	John Terrey	1
Jos: Mathews)	3	Wm Wyatt	1	Hen: Allen,ye bigest	1
Will, a negro)		Peter Walker	1	Widow Meers	4
Wm Daniel	2	John Collins	1	Edwd. Hichin	1
John Francklin	3	Wm Smith	1	Fran: Battson	2
Sebast: Delastatius	2	Thos: Cayle	1	David Griffin	2
Wm Anderson	14	Robt. Attkinson	1	John How	2
Edwd. Moore	2	John Melson	1	Wm Nock	2
Samuel Tayler	2	Wm Wright	1	Isaac Medcalfe	2
Wm Whittington	3	Max: Gore	--	John Michael	3
Robt. Moorecok	3	Wm Baugh	--	Hen: Lurton	1
John Francisco & wife)	3	Nicho: Edwards	--	Robt. Edge	1
Peter Morgan)		Jno. Deane	--	Richard Marriner	1
Nath: Ratcliff	3	Richard Hastings	1	Nath: Bradford	8
John Barrick	2	Richard Hill	2	Hen: Chancy	1
Wm Tailer, Sr.	6	Tho: Welburne	2	Ed: Burd	1
Wm Tailer, Jr.	4	Daniel Jenifer	19	Edm: Allin, Const:	2
Barnet Ramsee	1	John Lewis	1	Samuel Beech	2
Alex: Massy	1	Dennis Morris	2	John Cole	4
James Tailer	1	Morris Dennis	2	Jno. Willis	2
John Stratton	1	John Dyer	1	Wm Custis	6
Tho: Thomas	1			Edwd. Tatham	1
John Belley	1	Majr. Bowman's prsincts.		Wm Twford	1
Robt. Lambert	1	Wm Parker	2	Wm Burton	6
Joseph Basnet	1	Peter Parker	2		
Hen: Towles	1	Walter Harges	2	Capt. Johnson's List	
Tho: Smith	1	Jack, a negro at)		Fran: Roberts	3
Wm Jones	1	Adam Michaels)	1	Jno. Read	2
John Evans	1	Wm Pettijohn	1	Jno. Smith	1
Teage Miskell	1	Wm Johnson	1	Edwd. Ellis	1
Amos Cooke	1	Wm Marshall	2	Tho: Marshall	3
John Booth	1	Geo: Brown	3	Obe: Johnson	2
Tho: Leegh	1	Rich: Greenal	2	Tho: Johnson	3
Jno. Jackson	1	John Barnes	2	Will: Gouldin	1
Tho: Foster	1	Edwd. Bailey	2	Peter Dolby	1
Wm Blake, Sr.	1	Geo: Hope	3	James Camell	2
Wm Blake, Jr.	1	Rich: Bundick	3	Tho: Parremore,	
John Blake	1	John Sturgis	1	Constable	2
Wood: Stokeley	1	Thomas Crippin	3	Joseph Clarke	1
Wm Atkins	1	Edmd. Bowman	7	Tho: Clarke	2
Tob: Bull	1	Jno. Jnions	2	Rich: Garretson	2
Nath: Tunnell	1	Edwd. Gellson	1	Robt. Watson	4
Danl. Harwood	1	Isaac Dix	4	Simon Foster	1
James Davis	1	John Wheeler	1	Cornelius Harman	1
Robt Atkins	1			Charles Roberts	1
Edwd. Thorneton	1	Capt. Custis prsints.		Samuel Cobb	1
Fran: Stockley	1	John Bagwell	2	Robt. Wattson, Jr.	1
Wm Stockley	2	Tho: Bagwell	2	Arthur Robins	5

33

ACCOMACK TITHABLES (Tax Lists): 1663 - 1695

	Tithes		Tithes		Tithes
Jno. Clarke	1	Tho: Midleton	1	Jno. Fitzgarrel	1
Geo: Smith	4	Wm Andrews	2	Rawl Tanner	1
John Scamel	1	Jno. Roberts	1	John Wise, Sr.	9
Jno. Savage	1	Wm Fletcher	3	Wm Sill	1
John Shepperd	2	Wm Chace	2	James Ewell	1
Widow Jordan	1	Lancelot Jacquis		Cha: Leatherbury	3
Ralph Doe, Sr.	3	Jno. Holding	1	Cha: Scarburgh	10
John Hamering	1	Geo: Charnock	1	Peter Prichet, Sr.	2
Widow Jackson	4	Tho: Lucus	2	Joseph Ribinson	5
Fran: Wainehouse	1	James Smuthers	1	Tho: Fooks	2
David Gibins	1	Jno. Rowles	5		
Wm Bettes	1	Wm Pilcher	1	Capt. Hill prsincts:	
Edwd. Anthony	2	Tho: Bushell	5	Jno. Arew	1
Rich: Jacob	1	Nich: Dunn	1	Jno. Cary	1
		Robt. Huchinson	2	Jno. Lewis, Sr.	3
Mr. Bally's prsincs.		Abrah: Taylor	2	Jno. Lewis, Jr.	2
Edmd. Scarburgh	6	Jno. Chace	1	Tho: Rila	1
John Walthom	4	Hen: Read	5	Tho: Blake	2
Rich: Kellam, Sr.	3	James Longo	1	Wm Bunting	2
Clemt. Onley	1	Jno. Smally	1	Wm Denison	1
Saml. Serjent	1	Rich: Bally	3	Peter Clavell	1
Dormt. Sullivant	4	Abra: Tayler, Jr.	1	Arth: Frame	1
John Nellson	1	Geo: Nich: Hack	8	Wm Jarman	3
Hen: Hill	1	Ed: Kellam	1	Wm Silverthorne	2
Danl. Darby	1			Roger Ternan	1
Joseph Ames	2	Majr. Scarburgh's prscts.		Walter Warrington	1
Jno. Mecome	1	Edwd. Revell	5	John Baily	8
Mr. Tho: Teackle	3	John Parker, Sr.	4	John Abbot	2
Jno. Walker	1	Rich: Piwell	1	Tho: Webb	3
Peter Watkinson	1	Jno. Sharplys Tinker	4	Geo: Midleton	1
Jonath: Nuton	1	Jno. Jenkins, Sr.	5	Roger Miles	1
Wm Lingo	2	Jeremiah Perry	2	Jno. Tounsen	1
Jno. Parkes	2	Wm Phillips	2	Tho: Nickson	2
Jno. Spires	1	William Wale	1	Fran: Whorton	1
Tho: Willson	2	John Lewis	1	John Smith	2
Rich: Hoventon	1	Wm Thoroton	1	Ralph Justice	1
Geo: Ginn	1	And: Stopp	1	Geo: West	1
George Barlyman	1	Rich: Cutler	2	Robt: Burton	1
Rhod: Powell	1	John Kellam	1	Wonie Macklanie	2
Rich: Melton	1	James Foster	1	John Drumond	3
Wm White, Sr	2	Steph: Warrington	3	George Truit	2
Geo: Russell	2	Jno. Laws	3	Jno. Truit	1
Jno. Simcok	1	Morgan Licence	1	Jno. Ayres	2
Rowland Savage	4	Jno. Fenn	1	Rich: Hinman	3
Rich: Jones	2	Phill: Quinton	2	Jno. Hudson	1
Wm Smith	1	James Watkin	1	Nich: Newman	1
Jno. Washbourne	2	Tho: Barnet	1	Tho: Scot	3
Jno. Milby	1	Rich: Waring	1	Xophr: Thomson	1
Jos: Milby	2	Teage Andros	3	Robt. Hawlie	1
Alexander Richards	1	Wm Wise	1	Geo: Johnson	3
Owen Collonon, Sr.	4	Wm Mason	1	Tim: Coe	3
Rich: Niblet	1	Tho: Evans	1	John Gladding	1
Arnold Harrison	2	James Tissaker	1	Jno. Prettiman	2
Jno. Lecat	1	Hen: Gibbons	1	John West	16

ACCOMACK TITHABLES (Tax Lists): 1663 - 1695

	Tithes		Tithes		Tithes
John Brooks	4	Oliver Morgan	1	Danl. Ograyhan	2
Peter Morgan	1	Robt. Holliday	1		
Wm Wilson	1	Mr. Hack's boy	1		

Totall 638 - v. vi - pp. 386-388

The List of Tithables in Accomack County of ye yeare 1685

Capt. John Wallop's pcts		Jn Beasly.	1	John Onyons	3
Lt. Coll Danl. Jenifer	17	Wm Rust	1	John Wheelers	1
Mr. Wm Anderson	10	Thom Thomas	1	Rich: Greenall	2
Wm Tayler, Sr.	6	John Tounsend	1	Wm Martiall	3
Wm Brittingham	4	Francis Stockley	1	Wm Johnson	1
Wm Tayler, Jr.	4	James Davis	1	Rich: Bundick	2
Capt. Jno. Wallop	4	Joseph Stockley	1	Edwd. Bally	1
Guse: Vannetson	2	Danl. Harwood	1	Geo: Hope	4
Hen: Towles	2	Robt. Hill	1	Edmd. Bowman	7
Saml. Tayler	2	Robt. Halle	1	Wm Brown	1
John Francisco	2	Jno. Hudson	1	John Barnes	3
Wm Wright	2	Oliver Morgan	1		
James Tayler, Sr.	2	Roger Miles	1	Capt. Custis prcints.	
Wm Daniell	2	Jno. Evans	1	Wm Burton	5
Dorothy Watts	2	Robt. Farrington	1	Hen: Custis	2
Symon Smith	2	Rich: Haies	1	Wm Sacker	1
Dennis Morris	2	Fran: Wharton	1	James Walker	3
Wm Atkins	2	Jno. Bloxum	1	Hen: Williams	2
Nathl. Tunnell	2	Tho: Woosle	1	John Willis	2
Morris Dennis	2	Jonath: Owen	1	Edwd. Revell	4
Benjamin Eyres	2	Wm Shepherd	1	Isaac Medcalfe	2
Robt. Burton	2	Sebast: Delastatius	1	Robt. Sample	1
John Burrick	2	Alex: Mills	1	Edwd. Burd	1
Wood: Stockley	2	Peter Walker	1	Widow Mears	1
Tho: Tounsend	1	Barnet Ramsie	1	Tho: Mills	1
Jno. Gladding	1	Alex: Massie	3	Frans. Batteson	2
John Nellson	1	Wm Stockly	3	John Welch	1
Tobias Bull	1	Wm Blake	3	Walter Hargis	1
Robt. Atkinson	1	Jno. Moore	3	John Lawes	1
Mr. John Stratton	1	Nath: Ratcliff	3	Wm Finne	1
Wm Benston	1	Mr. Brooks	3	Rich: Marriner	1
Rich: Flowers	1	Geo: West	3	John Cole	4
John Tarr	1	Nich: Millechop	3	Wm Twyford	1
Edwd. Thornton	1	Isaac Dix	4	Hen: Chancy	1
Robt. Davis	1	Tho: Simpson	3	Rich: Garretson	1
Peter Bootie	1	Wm Parker	2	Ed: Hitchin	1
Peter Morgan	1	Tho: Crippin	3	Widow Michael	1
John Hancock	1	Peter Perker	2	Arth: Upshot	7
David Jones	1	Geo: Parker	2	Wm Nock	2
John Genner	1	John Wheeler	1	Hen: Lurton	1
Walter Mannington	1	John Sturgis	1	Robt. Edge	2

ACCOMACK TITHABLES (Tax Lists): 1663 - 1695

	Tithes
Tho: Bagwell	3
Jno. Will, Jr.	1
Nath: Bradford	10
Jno. Bagwell	3
Wm Custis	5
Capt. Johnson's prsct.	
John Shepherd	2
Tho: Tailer	1
Obed: Johnson	3
Saml. Cobb	1
Tho: Inoue	1
Cornel. Harman	1
Simon Foscue	1
Geo: Anthony	2
Robt. Tornion	2
James Scamell	1
John Read	1
John Smith	1
John Nussay	1
Widow Jackson	3
John Clarke	1
Wm Williams	1
Geo: Smith	3
Fran: Roberts	3
Robt. Watson	3
Tho: Parramore	4
Tho: Marshall	4
Fran: Wainhouse	1
Edm: Joyne	3
Robt. Watson, Jr.	1
Arth: Robins	7
Wm Betts	1
Edwd. Wheatcraft	1
Mr. Rich: Bally's prsct.	
Capt. Ed: Scarburgh	5
John Rowles	3
And: Steward	5
Dormt. Sullivant	3
Jno. Nellson	2
Hen: Hill	2
Jos: Ames	2
Peter Watkinson	2
Jno. Lecatt	2
Wm Andrews	2
Robt. Hutchinson	1
Ab: Tayler, Sr.	1
Ab: Tayler, Jr.	1
John Chace	1
Nich: Dunn	1
Jno. Holding	1
Tho: Midleton	1
James Longo	1

	Tithes
Daniel Darby	1
Rich: Jones	1
Hen: Stakes	1
Rich: Niblet	1
Peter Rogers	1
John Whitehead	1
David Gibbins	1
Saml. Serjent	1
Clemt. Only	1
Rich: Kellam	4
Row: Savage	3
John Major	2
John Sparkes	1
Wm Lingo	2
Wm Smith	1
Wm White	2
Owen Collonon	4
John Walthum	4
Joh: Milby	3
Geo: Russell	2
Rho: Powell	1
Rich: Melton	1
Tho: Willson	2
Rich: Hoveington	1
Geo: Ginn	1
Geo: Haselop	1
John Spires	1
Arnold Harrison	2
John Simcok	1
John Washbourne	3
Wm Fletcher	4
Mr. Teackle	3
Henry Read	5
Tho: Bushell	5
Hance Bettnor	2
John Smally	1
John Walker	1
Sanl. Ograyhan	2
Wm Golding	1
Rich: Bally	4
Mr. Hack's prsincts.	
Mrs. Matts	9
Teage Anderson	3
James Bonewell	3
Tho: Fooks	3
Steph: Warrington	3
Phill: Quinton	2
Rich: Cutler	2
James Ewell	2
Cha: Leatherbury	2
John Jenkins	5
John Parker, Sr.	6
Wm Phillipps	2

	Tithes
James Fooks	2
John Kellam	1
Wm Heath	1
Jos: Newton	1
John Chandler	1
John Richenson	1
Tho: Thornbury	1
Wm Wise	1
Tho: Evans	1
Hen: Gibbons	1
James Tissaker	1
Peter Pritchet	2
John Wise, Sr.	8
Wm Sill	1
Jno. Fitzgarrel	1
Paul Tanner	1
Jno. Fenn	2
John Lewis	1
Wm Thoroton	1
Andrew Stope	1
Rich: Piwell	1
Geo: Nich: Hack	8
Perry Leatherbury	2
Majr. Scarburgh	4
Capt. Hill's prsct.	
John Bayley	9
Ed: Brotherton	1
Peter Clevill	1
Ralph Justice	1
Arth: Frame	1
Tho: Webb	2
John Lewis, Sr.	3
Geo: Middleton	2
John Aires	2
Tho: Blake	3
John Drumond, Sr.	2
John Trewitt	2
Wony Macklanny	2
Tho: Scott	2
John Abbot	2
John Lewis, Jr.	1
Tho: Ryley	1
Wm Bunting	3
Geo: Johnson	2
Wm Silverthorne	2
Wm Jermon	1
John Arew	1
Roger Ternon	2
Nich: Newman	1
Xopher Tompson	1
Stephen Filby	1
Rich: Johnson's negro	1

ACCOMACK TITHABLES (Tax Lists): 1663 - 1695

	Tithes		Tithes		Tithes
Capt. Hill	3	Coll: John West	15	James Smothers	1
Timothy Coe	3	Capt. Whittington	3	Max: Gore	3
John Collins	1	Wm Waite	1	Rich: Hinman	2
Tho: Nixson	1	John Stanton	1	John Fisher	1
Wm Mason	1	Mr. Welburn	3	Cants. Bence	2
Mica Warder	1	Wm Tinly	1	Tho: Johnson	3
Co: Johnson	1	Geo: Dewy	3	Ralph Doe	1
John Hamering	1	Hen: Allin, Jr.	1	Mr. Saml. Sandford	3
James Truit	1	Nich: Hill	1		

The totll. 644 - v. vi - p. 414

The List of Tithables in Accomack County for A.D. 1686

	Tithes		Tithes		Tithes
Capt. Wallop's pcincts		Ben: Eyres	2	Nath: Ratcliff	3
John Wallop	3	Danl. Harwood	1	Wm Weight	1
Samuel Tailer	1	Jonath: Owen	1	Tho: Welburne	4
Max: Gore	4	Rich: Flowers	1	Wm Blake, Jr.	2
Nath: Tunnell	2	Morrice Dennis	1	Wm Blake, Sr.	1
James Davis	1	Rich: Hastings	2	Edwd. Carter	1
John Collins	1	Tho: Leigh	1	John Pretteman	1
Wm Atkins	1	Rich: Hayes	1	Oliver Morgan	1
Tho: Stockely	1	Robt. Farrington	1	Edwd. Moore, Jr.	1
Francis Stockley	1	Tho: Wheeler	1	Wm Benston, Sr.	1
Peter Walker	3	Tho: Tounsing	1	Alexandr. Massey	--
Simon Smith	1	Jno. Gladding	1	Robt. Atkins	1
Wm Wright	2	Rho: Talsby	1	John Welton	1
Edw: Thorneton	1	Peter Morgan	1	Wm Daniel	2
Jno. Francisco, negro	2	Sebast: Delastatius	3	James Tailer, Sr.	2
Jno. Hudson	1	Guslin Venetson	1	Barnet Ramse	1
Fran: Wharton	1	Hen: Brombill	1	John Ferrell	1
Christ: Hudder	1	Henry Toles	2	John Watts	4
John Melson	1	Tobius Bull	1	Nicho: Millechop	2
Jno. Bloxum	1	Wm Tailor, Jr.	5	Edwd. Bayly	2
Kanutus Bence	1	Wood: Stockley	4	Rich: Cooper	1
John Hancock	1	Wm Stockley	2	John Barrick	2

ACCOMACK TITHABLES (Tax Lists): 1663 - 1695

	Tithes		Tithes		Tithes
John Jackson	2	Wm Nock	4	John Savage	1
Geo: West	3	Hen: Chancy	1	Joseph Clarke	1
Roger Miles	2	Edwd. Burd	1	Tho: Clarke	2
Dennis Morris	3	John Willis	3	Frans. Roberts	3
Rich: Greenall	2	Edw. Revell	5	John Clarke	1
Wm Silverthorne, Sr.	2	Wm Burton	5	Geo: Smith	3
Saml. Sandford	2	John Pettejohn	2	Rich: Garritson	2
Thomas Thomas	1	Wm Custis	5	Robt. Watson, Jr.	1
Wm Whittington	5	Ann Cmichael	1		
Danl. Jenifer	15	Robt. Watson	1	Mr. Baily's prcincts	
Robt. Barton	2	Nathl. Bradford	10	Robt. Hutchinson	4
George Hope	5	Tho: Bagwell	5	Abraham Tayler,Sr.	2
Wm Anderson	17	Rich: Marriner	1	Abraham Tayler,Jr.	1
William Smith	2	Saml. Beech	1	Tho: Middleton	1
Wm Brittingham	6	Robt. Taylor	1	Jno. Charles	1
John Custis	3	John Bagwell	1	Danl. Ograyhan	2
Wm Howard	1	Wm Twyford	1	Wm Walle	1
John Wimbrow	1	Hen: Lurton	1	Hen: Read	4
Wm Shepard	1	Griffin Evins	1	Rowland Savage	3
Peter Booten	1	Edwd. Hichin	1	Rich: Jones	1
John Jones	1	Robt. Sempler	1	John Chace	1
Wm Merrell	1	Wm Jones	1	John Rowles	2
Robin Davis	2	Arthr. Upshor	--	Hared Betner	1
				James Chapman	1
Majr. Bowman's prcincts		Capt. Johnson's prcincts		Rich: Hoventon	1
Wm Perker	2	Obed: Johnson	4	Saml. Serjent	1
Tho: Simson	3	Simon Foscue	3	Tho: Bushell	4
Wm Bunting	3	Samll Cobb	1	Geo: Charnock	1
John Onions	2	Joshua Cobb	1	Jno. Houlding	1
Rich: Bundick	2	John Cobb, Const:	1	Wm Pilcher	1
James Furbush	1	Geo: Dewy	2	Jno. Walker	2
John Wheeler	1	Tho: Johnson	2	Wm Andrews	3
Isa: Dix	5	Geo: Anthony	1	Jno. Smally	1
Robt. Holliday	2	Math: Lailor	1	Wm Alford	1
John Barnes	2	Cornelius Johnson	1	Nich: Dunn	1
Geo: Parker	3	Tho: Parramore, Const:	4	Jno. Washbourne	3
Peter Parker	3	James Camell	1	James Longo	3
Edmund Bowman	7	John Hamering	2	Daniel Darby	2
Tho: Criping	2	Robt. Briggs	2	Wm Fletcher	3
Wm Browne, Sr.	1	Ralph Doe, Sr.	2	Owen Collonon	4
Henry Ubanck	1	Tho: Marshall	4	Rich: Niblet	3
Wm Johnson	1	John Johnson	2	Arnold Harrison	1
Wm Marshall	3	Lidia Jackson	3	David Gibbons	1
		Arthur Robins	7	John Major	2
Capt. Custis prcincts		Tho: Taylor	1	Clemt. Only	1
James Walker Sr.	2	Jno. Smith, Sr.	1	Edmd. Scarburgh	5
Robt. Walker	2	John Read	2	Tho: Teackle	6
Hen: Custis	3	Cornelius Harmanson	1	Will: Milby	2
John Welch	1	Tho: Lucus	1	Joseph Milby	1
Hen: Allin ye bigger	--	John Shepherd	1	John Milby	2
Walter Hargis	1	Will: Gouldin	1	Geo: Russell	2
John Cole	2	Wm Heath	1	John Simcock	1
Isaac Medcalfe	3	Francis Wainhouse	1	Wm White	2
Hen: Williams	2	Robt. Watson, Sr.	4	Rich: Melton	1

ACCOMACK TITHABLES (Tax Lists): 1663 - 1695

Name	Tithes	Name	Tithes	Name	Tithes
Rhod Powell	1	Daniel Byles	1	Jno. Stratton	1
John Waltham	5	John Lecatt	1	Wm Tayler, Sr.	5
Rich: Kellam, Sr.	4	James Gray	2		
Andrew Steward	4	Joseph Ames	1	The Totall of ye	
Dormt. Sullivant	2	Peter Watkinson	1	Tithbles. 705	
John Nelson	1	Rich: Piwell	1		
Hen: Hill	2	Peter Pritchet	2	v. vi - p. 437	
Arthur Gale (Gall?)	1	John Wise	8		
Saml Doe	2	Geo: Nich: Hack	7		
Robt. Monke	1	Wm Sill	1		
Geo: Ginn	2				
Tho: Wilson	2	Capt. Hill's prcincts			
Jno. Spires	1	Rich: Hinman	2		
Wm Lingo	2	Wm Jerman	3		
Rich: Bally	5	Jno. Carie	1		
Jno. Sparkes	2	Morgan Jones	2		
Geo: Hazelup	4	John Truit	1		
Edwd. Gilson	1	Robt. Hallie	1		
		Tho: Blake	2		
Mr. Hack's prcincts		John Lewis, Jr.	2		
Cha: Scarburgh	13	Tho: Scot	1		
John Parker	7	John Lewis, Sr.	4		
John Lewis	1	Tho: Nixson	1		
Wm Thornton	1	Hen: Dighton	1		
Joseph Newton	1	Roger Ternan	2		
Saml. Fittiman	2	Peter Clavell	1		
John Chandler	1	Jno. Arew	1		
John Richardson	1	Jno. Ayres	3		
John Fitzgerrald	3	Xopr. Thomson	2		
Andrew Stop	1	Rich: Johnson	1		
Perry Leatherbury	2	Arthur Frame	1		
John Fisher	1	John Stanton	1		
Robert West	1	Stephen Philby	1		
Wm Phillips	2	Jno. Baily	5		
Geo: Davis	1	Jno. Drumond	3		
John Fenn	1	Wony Macklanny	3		
James Bonewell	3	James Truit	2		
Wm Poaper	2	Timo: Coe	4		
Tho: Thornbury	1	Tho: Webb	2		
Cha: Leatherbury	2	John Abbot	2		
Wm Mason	1	Ed: Barrat	1		
Teague Andros	2	Geo: Midleton	2		
Geo: Parker	5	Ralph Justice	1		
Joseph Robinson	3	Rich: Hill	4		
Wm Finne	2	Coll West	17		
James Ewell	1	Edwd. Kellam	2		
James Tisseker	1	Hen: Gibbons	1		
Wm Wise	1	Jno. Rogers	1		
Paul Tanner	1	Wm Pritchet	1		
Stevan Warrington	2	Geo: Johnson	3		
Alexandr. Harrison	2	Tho: Cartwraight	1		
Tho: Foolkes	2	Tho: Gothogon	1		
John Lawes	1	Richard Cutler	2		
John Jenkins	4	David Thomas	1		

ACCOMACK TITHABLES (Tax Lists): 1663 - 1695

The List of Tithables for Accomack County for A.D. 1687

	Tithes		Tithes		Tithes
Capt. Wallop pcints					
Lt Col Danl. Jenefer	15	Tho. Lee	1	Edw. Brotherton	3
Capt. Wm Whittington	5	Francis Stockly	2	Roger Miles	2
Geo: Blake	4	Wm Wright	1		
Capt. Jno. Wallop	3	Jno. Gladwin	1	Capt. Custis pcints.	
John Hooton	4	Jno. Hodeson	1	Arthur Upshore	7
Wm Page	1	Mr. Jno. Stratton	1	Wm Nock	4
Wm Merrill	1	Jos: Newton	1	Jno. Willis	3
Richard Sanders	1	Wm Daniel	2	Hen: Chancy	1
John Onions	1	Wm Waite	1	Hen: Lurton	1
Wm Smith	2	Peter Bow----	1	Robt. Tayler	1
Isaack Dix	4	James Davis	1	Hen: Williams	3
Winifred Parker	4	Nath: Radeliff	2	James Walker	2
James Taylor	1	Nath: Tunnell	2	Rich: Marriner	1
John Farrell	1	Alexr. Masse	3	Tho: Francklin	1
Dennis Morris	2	Jno. Beesly	1	Rich: Garritson	3
Morris Denas	1	James Tayler, Sr.	1	Edw: Hitchins	2
Daniel Harwood	1	Alexandr. Benston	1	Saml. Beech	1
Wm Taylor	3	Barnard Ramsie	1	Ann Michael	4
John Bonner	1	Peter Clavill	1	Edw. Allen	1
John Hancock	1	Geo: West	2	Jno. Welch	1
Jno. Popelwell	1	Thomas Thomas	1	Bart: Meers	2
Wm Atkins	1	Rich: Gesture	3	Nath: Bradford	7
Jno. Collins	1	Jno. Bloxum	1	Wm Burton	4
Jno. Stockley	1	Wm Benston, Sr.	1	Wm Twiford	2
Mr. Tho: Welburne	5	Rich: Hargos	1	Robt. Edge	1
Jno. Francisco	3	Tho: Touning	1	Wm Custis	5
Peter Walker	3	Rich: Hasting	2	Hen: Custis	4
Geo: Hope	4	Henery Towles	1	Hen: Allen	1
Jno. Mellson	1	Roger Selings	1	Wm Pettejohn	2
Jno. Jones	1	Maxa: Gore	7	Hen: Stakes	1
James Forbus	1	Jno. Barrick	2	Edwd. Burd	1
Wm Paine	1	Edw: Moore	1	Francis Sacker	1
Rich: Greenell	2	Olivr. Morgan	1	Jno. Cole	2
Nich: Millechop	1	Jno. Watts	3	Robt. Sample	1
Simon Smith	1	Wm Brittingham	6	Tho: Wilkinson	1
Samll. Sanford	1	Wm Benston, Jr.	1	Tho: Bagwell	4
Richd. Cooper	1	Robt. Atkins	1	Isaac Medcalfe	1
Samll. Cobb	1	Jno. Willton	1	Walter Hargis	1
Jno. Jacson	1	Tho. Wheeler	1	David Griffin	1
Kan: Bence	1	Jonathan Owen	1	Wm Parker	2
Elias Tayler	4	Wm Blake, Sr.	3	Wm Grooten	1
Tho: Perry	2	Rich: Bundick	2	Tho: Bowles	1
Tho: Stockly	1	Jacob Waggaman	1		
Wm Lucus	1	Geo: Johnson	5	Capt. Johnson's	
Jno. Blake	2	Fran: Allixander	2	pcints	
Francis Wharton	1	Jno. Wheeler	1	Jno. Newman	3
Wm Silverthorne	3	Ralph Justice	2	Tho: Marshall	4
Rich: Price	2	Walter Lane	1	Jno. Greeke	1
Robt. Hill	2	Robt. Burton	2	James Camell	1
Rich: Flower	2	Jno. Custis	7	Jno. Smith	1
Guslin Venetson	1	Robt. Davis	2	Jno. Read	1

ACCOMACK TITHABLES (Tax Lists): 1663 - 1695

Name	Tithes	Name	Tithes	Name	Tithes
Ralph Doe, Sr.	2	Rich: Niblet	2	Tho: Blake	2
Widdow Johnson	5	Jno. Simcock	2	Jno. Littleton	1
Fran: Wainhous	1	Wm White	2	Geo: Parker	3
Tho: Johnson	2	Wm Lingo	1	Jno. Barnes	2
Jno. Shepherd	1	Owen Collonon	5	Rich: Sturgis	1
Jno. Savage	2	Jno. Sparkes	2	Tho: Crippin	3
Geo: Smith	2	Jno. Spires	1	Rich: Hinman	3
Jno. Rogers	2	Tho: Willson	1	Wm Willet	2
Fran: Roberts	3	Tho: Allum	1	Fran: Cooke	1
Robt. Samson	1	Jno. Walthom	3	Jno. Ayres, Sr.	3
Jno. Clarke	1	Jno. Major	2	Ed: Baly	1
Tho: Tayler	1	Saml. Doe	3	Wm Johnson	1
Joseph Cobb	1	Obed: Andrews	1	Jno. Cary	1
Samll Banton	1	Jno. Smally	2	Tho: Simson	4
Simon Foscue	2	Wm Fletcher	3	Jno. Lewis	5
Robt. Thomson	2	Jno. Walker	3	Wm Bunting	3
Wm Betts	1	Jo: Milby	1	Roger Ternan	2
Geo: Hinton	1	Jno. Milby	2	Wm Denison	1
Cornell: Harmanson	1	James Longo	1	Jno. Hornbie	1
Jo: Clarke	1	Clemt. Golding	1	Jno. Abbot	3
Tho: Clarke	2	And: Steward	2	Jno. Arew	1
Robt. Watson, Jr.	2	Dormt. Sullivant	3	James Truit	3
Robt. Watson, Sr.	5	Jno. Nelson	1	Tho: Rilie	2
Geo: Duey	2	Hen: Hill	2	Tho: Nickson	1
Peter Watson	2	Jno. Alford	1	Wm Jarman	2
Howl. Francis	1	Geo: Haselop	1	Tho: Gogahan	2
Wm Kellam	2	Jno. Holding	1	Arth: Frame	1
Geo: Anthony	1	Geo: Charnock	1	Geo: Middleton	2
Jno. Hamering	2	Sam: Serjent	1	Wm Ballard	1
Math: Lailor	1	Jno. Washbourne	3	Martian Jones	2
Ath: Gall	1	Mr. Teacle	7	Wm Shore	1
Jno. Warrin	1	Rich: Kellam	4	Jno. Drumond	4
Rich: Jacob	1	Edw: Kellam	2	Robt. Burtne	1
Mr. Arthr. Robins	6	Hen: Sellman	1	Wm Souses	1
Tho: Parrimoore	4	James Chapman	1	Tho: Jenkins	1
Robt. Griggs	2	Nicho: Dun	1	Jno. Bally	6
Edm: Joynes	4	Tho: Middleton	2	Jno. Stanton	1
		Jno. Charles	1	Wm Marshall	2
Mr. Bally's pcints		Arnold Harrison	1	Rich: Johnsons	2
Mr. Ed: Scarburgh	6	Wm Pilcher	1	Wm Brown, Sr.	1
Abr: Taylor	2	Jno. Chase	1	Edm: Bowman	8
Robt. Monke	1	Jno. Tayler	1	Rich: Hill	4
Nath: Littleton	4	David Gibbins	1	Timothy Coe	3
Petr. Watkinson	1	Robt. Hutchinson	3		
James Gray	2	Tho: Bushell	2	Majr. Scarburgh's pcincts	
Danl. Darby	2	Jno. Rowles	3		
Jo: Ames	1	Wm Wale	1	Jno. Fenn	4
Jno. Lecatt	1	Danl Ogragon	2	Jno. Lewis	1
Rich: Jones	1	David Thomas	1	Morgn. Lizium	1
Rowland Savage	1	Mr. Rich: Bally	8	Wm Thoroton	1
Wm Milby	1	Mr. Geo: Nicho: Hack	9	Andrew Stopp	1
Rich: Hovengton	1			Wm Rawlins	1
Geo: Ginn	1	Capt. Hill's pcints		Tho: Scott	1
Rich: Melton	1	Chris: Thomson	3	Geo: Davis	1

41

ACCOMACK TITHABLES (Tax Lists): 1663 - 1695

The List of Tithables for Accomack County for A.D. 1688

Name	Tithes
Saml. Fittiman	1
John Morgan	1
Micha: Wardle	1
Wm Mason	1
James Fairfax	1
Alex: Harrison	2
Arth: Donis	1
Tho: Fooks	2
Rich: Cutler	2
Jno. Parker	7
Xpher Chippington	1
Wm Phillips	2
Valent. Mathews	6
Nath: Bradford, Jr.	3
James Euells	2
Jno. Richardson	1
John Huton	1
James Bonwell	2
John Lawes	1
Florence Matts	8
Wm Wale	2
Wm Wise	2
James Tisaker	1
Teage Andros	1
John Fisher	1
Jno. Lillingstone	1
Robt. West	1
Jno. Chandler	1
Joseph Ribinson	1
Jno. Jenkins	2
Cha: Leatherbury	2
Perry Leatherbury	2
Edwd: Revell	6
Hen: Gibbons	1
Tho: Evans	1
Tho: Farnbery	1
Jno. Wite	6
Wm Sill	1
Hen: Read	4
Peter Prichard	3
Jno. West	17
Cha: Scarbrough	11
Nich: Hill	1
Jno. Furs	1
Wm Hickman	1
Ye totall of tythes	744

v. vi - p. 460

Capt. Wallops prcts.

Name	Tithes
Joseph Newton	3
Mr. Sandford	2
Wm Brittingham	7
Jno. Wimburrow	1
Wm Tayler	4
Wm Wright	1
Saml. Tayler	4
James Powell	1
Hen: Towles	1
John Francisco	2
Hen: Rogers	1
Elias Tayler	4
Robt. Burton	1
Tho: Leigh	)
Danl. Cartee	) 2
Jonath: Owen	1
Wood: Stockley	3
Rich: Hastings	1
Danl. Harwood	1
Geo: Hope	5
At Mar: Eyres	1
Jacob Waggaman	1
John Stockly	1
Nathl. Ratcliff	1
At Morris Dennis	2
Wm Blake, Jr.	2
James Tayler	2
Alex: Massy	5
Rich: Flowers	1
John Watts	3
Wm Atkins	2
Dennis Morris	2
Edward Moore	1
Oliver Morgan	1
Wm Shepherd	1
Jno. Glading	1
James Davis	1
Nich: Millechop	2
John Lewcus	1
John Tounsend	1
Peter Booty	1
Wm Daniel	2
John Jackson	1
John Wallop	6
Sebat Delastatius	2
Tho: Tounsend	1
James Cudde	1
John Custis	7
Robt. Atkins	1
Jno. Wheelton	1
Tho: Conway	1

Name	Tithes
Garret Supple	2
Guslin Venelson	2
Frans. Stockley	1
Peter Walker	4
Tho: Welburne	5
John Collins	1
Tho: Perry	2
Edwd. Thorneton	1
Jona. Aileworth	1
James Smothers	1
John Hancok	1
John Bloxam	1
Rich: Jester	4
Peter Morgan	1
John Prettiman	2
Francis Moore	2
Geo: Ginn	1
Wm Paine	1
Wm Weight	1
Cha: Stockley	1
Tho: Tou----	1
Wm Benston	1
Tho: Gillet	1
Max: Gore	5
John Hudson	2
Geo: West	3
Tho: Stockley	2
Nath: Tunnell	1
Wm Blake, Senr	3
Danl. Jenifer	14
Hen: Brombill	1
Wm Anderson	16
Wm Benston, Sr.	2
Rich: Cooper	1

Capt. Hills prcints

Name	Tithes
Arth: Frame	1
Christ: Thomson	2
Rich: Bundick	1
Frans. Wharton	3
Edwd. Brotherton	2
Rich: Greenall	3
Robt. James	1
Edward Baily	2
James Furbush	1
Tho: Cripen	3
John Sturgis	1
John Baily	6
James Trewet	1
John Arew	1
Tho: Nickson	1

ACCOMACK TITHABLES (Tax Lists): 1663 - 1695

Name	Tithes	Name	Tithes	Name	Tithes
Tho: Gohogon	1	Capt. Custis prcts.		Rowld Savage	2
Rich: Sturgis	1	Wm Custis	6	Jos: Ames	--
Geo: Parker	2	John Rogers	2	James Gray	1
Wm Parker	2	Henry Custis	3	Mr. Teackle	7
Wm Brown, Sr.	2	John Revell	5	John Simcock	2
Wm Daniel	1	Rich: Marriner	3	Teackle Walthom	1
Tho: Jenkins	2	Robt. Edge	1	John Walthom	3
Rich: Johnson	2	Edwd. Hitchin	1	Rich: Kellam	5
John Wheeler	3	Widow Meers	3	And: Steward	2
Peter Clavill	1	Rich: Garretson	2	Dormt. Sullivant	2
Wm Thorne	1	Hen: Lurton	1	John Nelson	1
Frans. Aires	1	James Buton	1	Hen: Hill	2
John Lewis, Sr.	4	John Willis	3	Wm Goulding	1
Ralph Justice	2	Wm Nock	3	Jno. Milby	2
Rowld. Price	1	Walter Hargis	1	Jos: Milby	2
Robt. Haly	1	Widow Michael	3	Widow Major	1
Isaac Glover	1	Tho: Bagwell	5	Owen Collonon	5
Lewis Knight	1	Arth: Upshot	8	Rich: Niblet	1
Wm Ballard	1	Rich: Jacob	1	Wm Page	1
Tho: Oryly, Sr.	2	Nath: Bradford	12	John Walker	3
Wm Hutson	4	John Pettejohn	3	Wm Fletcher	4
Wm Bunting	3	David Griffin	2	Jno. Smally	1
John Onions	1	Tho: Francklin	1	Obed: Andrews	1
James Addison	2	Tho: Ironmonger	2	Wm Andrews	1
Tho: Dowell	2	Isaac Medcalfe	3	Wm Pilcher	1
Geo: Middleton	2	James Walker	4	John Chace	1
Hen: Hubanck	1	Hen: Chancy	2	Danl. Darby	3
Wm Groten	3	Wm Twyford	1	Peter Rogers	1
Wm Richards	1	Saml. Beech	1	Nath: Littleton	4
Roger Ternall	2	Robt. Tayler	1	Mich: Ricketts	1
John Carey	2	Ed: Kellam	3	John Rowles	4
Roger Miles	2	John Terry	1	Geo: Charnock	1
John Littleton	2	Hen: Stakes	1	Rich: Hoveington	1
James Ewell	2	Ed: Burd	1	Hen: Selman	1
Frans. Cook	1	Wm Burton	4	James Chapman	1
Richd. Hinman	2	Ed: Allen	1	Nick: Dunn	1
John Ellet	1	Wm Yeo	2	Geo: Nich: Hack	8
Wm Martiall	2	Tho: Milles	1	Jno. Washbourne	5
Jo: Thorne	1	Ed: Burk	1	Wm Wale	1
Jo: Woodland	1	John Cole	1	Robt. Hutchinson	3
Ed: Right	1			John Tayler	2
Tho: Simson	5	Mr. Baylys prcincts		Tho: Middleton	1
Tho: Blake	2	Edmd. Scarburgh	7	John Charles	2
Tho: Webb	1	John Sparks	2	Ab: Tayler, Jr.	1
Wm Willet	2	Robt. Monk	1	John Lecatt	2
Wm Shere	1	Tho: Willson	2	Danl. Ograyhan	2
Wm Jerman	2	John Spires	2	James Longo	1
John Abbot	4	Rich: Melton	1	Wm Alford	1
John Drumond	3	Tho: Allom	1	John Furs	1
Rich: Drumond	6	Tho: Burrows	1	Rich: Bally	6
Wm Litchfield	1	Rich: Jones	1	David Gibbons	1
Xopr. Hudder	1	Arnold Harrison	1	Robt. Watson	5
Geo: Johnson	5	Wm White	2	Fran: Robins	2
Tim: Coe	2	Geo: Hazelop	1	Wm Betts	1

ACCOMACK TITHABLES (Tax Lists): 1663 - 1695

Name	Tithes	Name	Tithes	Name	Tithes
Geo: Smith	3	John Parker, Sr.	7		
Peter Watson	1	John Lilliston	1		
Fran: Wainhouse	2	Xopr. Chippendale	1		
Simon Foskue	2	Barna: Oheavens	1		
Cornls. Harman	1	John Fisher	1		
Tho: Clarke	1	Wm Rawlins	1		
Robt. Thomson	2	John Wise, Sr.	8		
Hen: Floyd	1	Rich: Cutler	2		
Joseph Clark	1	John Burrock	1		
John Clark	1	Peter Pritchard	3		
John Savage	3	Hen: Read	3		
Wm Kellam	2	Cha: Leatherbury	2		
Wm Lingo	1	Cha: Scarburgh	12		
Howl. Francis	2	John West	16		
John Barker	1	Tho: Bushell	1		
Capt. James	3	Tully Robinson	3		
		Wm Wise	1		
Majr. Scarburgh prcts.					
John Lewis	1	The Totll. is 719 Tithbls.			
John Alford	1				
Danl. Byles	1	v. vi - p. 485			
And: Stop	1				
Wm Thoroton	1				
Tho: Scott	1	The List of Tithables for Accomack			
Steph: Warrington	2	County for A.D. 1689			
Arth: Donis	1				
Alexandr. Harrison	2	Capt. Wallops prcincts		Jonath: Owen	1
Wm Sill	1	Tho: Perry	1	Wm Blake, Sr	3
Tho: Fooks	2	Samuel Tayler, Sr.	4	Hen: Brombill	1
John Lawes	1	Woo: Stockley	3	Jno. Morris	1
David Nellson	2	John Watts	3	Alexdr. Massie	3
John Huton	1	Jno. Wallop	5	Wm Atkins	2
John Jenkins	4	Wm Peterson	1	Jno. Farrell	1
John Stanton	2	Daniel Harwood	2	Rich: Flowers	1
Frans. Mackenny	3	Peter Booty	1	James Tailer, Sr.	1
Teage Andros	2	Rich: Hastings	1	James Tailer, Jr.	1
Henry Gibbons	1	Wm Blake, Jr.	2	John Robts.shoomkr	1
Joseph Robinson	4	Jacob Waggaman	1	Jo: Newton	2
Geo: Parker	9	Max: Gore	6	James Powell	1
Wm Phillips	1	Alexdr. Goold at Mr)		Wm Slaterfeild	2
James Bonewell	2	Gores)	1	Jno. Stratton	1
John Fenn	4	John Stockley	2	Jno. Hudson	2
Robert West	1	Jos: Stockley	1	Rich: Jester	3
John Chandler	1	Frans. Stockley	1	Geo: West	1
John Allson	1	Tho: Stockley	1	Robert West	1
John Richardson	1	Wm Tayler	4	Tho: West	1
John Morgan	1	Elias Tayler	4	Rich: Holleway	1
Geo: Davis	1	Nath: Ratcliff	2	Hen: Brooks	1
Perry Leatherbury	3	Tho: Wheeler	1	Robt. Atkins	1
James Tisaker	1	John Francisco	2	Jno. Wheelton	1
Tho: Evans	1	Hen: Rogers	1	Tho: Gillet	1
Tho: Thorneberry	1	Wm Paine	1	Jno. Onyons	1
Wm Mason	1	Wm Whright	1	Edwd. Thoroton	1
Tho: Watkins	1	Nathl. Tunnell	2	Hen: Toules	1

ACCOMACK TITHABLES (Tax Lists): 1663 - 1695

Name	Tithes	Name	Tithes	Name	Tithes
James Davis	1	Saml. Fittiman	1	James Lurton	1
Nich: Millechop	3	Rich: Bundick	2	James Walker	3
Peter Morgan	1	Morgan Lawrence	1	Jno. Willis	2
Wm Lucus	1	James Atkinson	1	Jno. Willis, Jr.	1
Jno. Tounsen	1	Wm Johnson	1	Mordica Edwards	3
Jno. Hancok	1	Wm Bunting	2	Rich: Marriner	3
Jno. Bloxum	1	Wm Marshall	2	Jno. Rogers	2
Dennis Morris	1	Tho: Simson	5	Saml. Beech	1
Wm Brittingham	6	Tho: Crippen	2	Hen: Stakes	1
Gusalin Vannelson	2	Jno. Lewis, Sr.	--	Jno. Charles	1
Wm Daniel	3	Roger Ternal	2	Cha: Colvert	1
Jno. Prettiman	2	John Wheeler	3	Wm Tilney	1
Edwd. Moore	1	James Forbes	1	Jno. Williams	1
Geo. Ginn	1	Jno. Cole	3	Walter Harges	2
Vincent Langford	1	Rich: Greenall	3	Tho: Bagwell	5
Jonath: Aleworth	1	Humphry Milles	1	Wm Jerman	3
Frans: Moore	2	Francis Johnson	1	Edmd. Allin,Constbl	1
Oliver Morgan	1	John Sturgis	1	Jno. Welch	1
Jeremia Wood	1	Isac Glover	1	Lance Sanckhills	1
Wm Merrill	1	Geo: Midleton	1	Tho: Mills	1
Simon Smith	1	Peter Clavil	1	Perry Leatherby	2
Jno. Beasly	1	Robt. Abbot	1	Edwd. Kellam	4
Jno. Booth	2	Jno. Abbot, Sr.	3	Jno. Parker, Sr.	10
Jno. Custis	4	Wm Groten	4	Wm Kellam	2
Jno. Daniel	4	Tho: Ryly	2	Rich: Garritson	2
Geo: Hope	5	Fran: Ayres	2	Wm Lingo	1
Peter Walker	3	Edmd. Bowman	6	Tho: Ironmonger	1
Tho: Huget	1	Wm Willet	2	Wm Custis	6
Wm Anderson	14	Wm Litchfield	1	Nath: Bradford	8
Danl. Jenifer	13	James Ewell	3	Rich: Hinman	2
Frans. Whorton	3	Jno. Carey	2	Widow Coe	1
Richard Hare	2	Edwd. Gellson	1	Robt. Davis	2
Tho: Jones	1			Ed: Brotherton	3
Wm Waite	1	Capt. Wm Custis prcts		Tho: Ginkins	1
		Arthur Upshur	6	Jno. Rou	1
Majr. Bowman's prcts		Ann Michael	3	Rich: Hill	4
Robt. Bayly	2	Wm Burton	6	Job Truit	2
Roger Miles	1	David Griffin	1	James Truit	1
Arth: Frame	1	Fran: Croston	2	Wm Ballard	1
Rich: Price	1	John Pettijohn	3	Ralph Justis	2
Robt. Stanly	1	Ann Mecale	)	Tho: Jones	1
Lewis Knight	1	Tho: Nightingale)	1	Ed: Burke	1
Geo: Parker	1	Tho: Franklin	1	Jno. Drumond	3
Jno. Ellit	1	Hen: Allen ye less	1	Geo: Johnson	4
Jo: Thorne	1	Jno. Perry	1		
Wm Hudson	4	Jno. Revell	4	Mr. Robinsons prcts	
Robt. Barton	2	Widdow Meers	2	John West	8
Tho: Jenkins	1	Edwd. Burd	2	Anth: West	6
Wm Daniel	2	Edwd. Hitchin	2	Robert West	2
Julian Martin	1	Tho: Tayler	3	Nich: Hill	2
Jos: Woodland	2	Wm Nock	4	Peter Pritchard	2
Jno. Jones	1	Hen: Chancey	1	Tho: Blake	1
Wm Browne	1	Robt. Tayler	1	Peter Pritchard,Jr	1
Xopr. Thomson	2	Hen: Lurton	1	Jno. Fenn	2

ACCOMACK TITHABLES (Tax Lists): 1663 - 1695

Name	Tithes	Name	Tithes	Name	Tithes
Jno. Fisher	1	Peter Rogers	2	Jno. Barker	1
Jos: Hooke	1	Obed: Andrews	2	Jno. Rowles	2
Tho: Scott	1	Jno. Major	2	David Gibbons	1
James Bonewell	2	Jno. Milby	2	Jno. Savage	3
Tho: Farmbrugh	1	Abra: Tayler, Sr.	2	Wm. Betes	1
Wm Wise	1	Tho: Allum	1	Simon Foscue	2
Tully Robinson	2	Mikell Rickards	2	Cornelius Harman	1
Cha: Leatherbury	3	Tho: Burrows	1	Rowld. Savage	1
Jno. Alfred	1	Wm Alford	1	Rich: Jones	1
Danl. Byles	1	Tho: Midleton	2	Rich: Niblet	2
Arth: Donis	3	Jno. Nelson	1	Jno. Walker	1
David Nelson	2	Wm Golding	1	Rich: Rogers	1
Jno. Chandler	1	Wm Heath	1	Bowman Littleton	2
Wm Phillips	1	Danl. Darby	3	Tho: Williams	1
Steph: Warrington,		At James Gray's	2	Wm Page	1
Constble	3	Wm Andrews	1	Rich: Bally	5
Jno. Stanton	3	Rich: Kellam, Sr.	2	Wm Wale	1
Teige Anderson	2	Rich: Kellam, Jr.	2	Wm Mason	1
James Tusszacar	1	Jno. Parkes	2		
Paul Tanner	1	Wm White, Sr.	3	Added at ye Levy	
Hen: Gibbons	1	Geo: Hazelup	1	Tho: Welburne	3
Jno. Laws	1	Jno. Spires	2	Geo: Nich: Hack	9
Jno. Burrock	1	Jno. Washbourne	2	Mr. James Tithbls.	4
John Jenkins	4	James Longo	1	Jno. Barnes	2
Rich: Cutler	1	Tho: Willson	1	Tho: Tounsend	1
Jno. Baily	6	Owen Collonon	5	Tho: Webb	1
Fran: Cooke	2	Wm Sill	1	Jno. Littleton	1
George Parker	9	Robt. Munck	1	Saml. Sandford	6
Jno. Morgan	1	Arnold Harrison	2	Francis Wharton	3
Jno. Richardson	1	Rich: Melton	1	Rich: Haze)	
Geo: Davis	1	Teackle Walthum	1	Robt: Jarvis)	2
Tho: Fooks	3	Jno. Walthum	3	Tho: Jones	1
Alex: Harrison	2	Jno. Simcock	2	Rich: Cooper	1
Tho: Tayler, Cooper	1	Wm Fletcher	2		
Patrick ye Miller	1	Jno. Lecatt	2	723 Totll. tith-	
Rich: Butler	1	Wm Pilcher	1	ables	
Jos: Robinson	2	Jno. Tayler	1		
Bryan Pert	3	Rich: Hoveington	1	v. vi - p. 519	
Wm Thoroton	2	Geo: Charnock	1		
And: Stop	1	Hen: Selman	1		
Jno. Wise, Sr.	7	James Chapman	1		
Fran: Mackenny	5	Nich: Dunn	1		
Hen: Read	8	And: Steward	4		
Cha: Scarburgh	11	Dormt. Sullivant	3		
Danl. Ograyhan	2	Robt. Watson	5		
		Fran: Wainhouse	3		
Mr. Ballys prcincts		Robt. Watson, Jr	1		
Ed: Scarburgh	6	Joseph Ames	1		
Tho: T°ackle	6	Peter Watson	1		
Alexdr. Richards	1	Francis Roberts	2		
Jos: Milby	3	Robt: Thomson	2		
Robt. Hutchinson	3	Jos: Clarke	1		
Rich: Hill	1	Tho: Clarke	2		
Jno. Chace	2	Geo: Smith	3		

ACCOMACK TITHABLES (Tax Lists): 1663 - 1695

A List of tithables in Accomack county for the Yeare 1690

	Tithes		Tithes		Tithes
Mr. Tho: Welburne his precincts		Morgan Liston	1	Jno. Wimburrow	1
		James Hartley	1	Robt. Burton	1
Jo: Stockley	2	Anth: Gerrard	1	Majr. Bowmans prcts.	
Tho: Stockely	2	Robt. West	1	Jno. Jones	2
Tho: Perrey	1	Wm Anderson	11	Jno. Cole	2
Jno. Gladding	2	Lewis Knight	2	Jno. Doe	1
James Smothers	1	Fran: Stockley	2	Hen: Hubanck	1
Saml. Sandford	6	James Powell	1	Edwd. Gellson	1
James Davis	1	Wm Pattison	1	Tho: Mills	2
Jno. Stockley	2	Jno. Collins	1	Jno. Abbot, Sr.	2
Peter Walker	3	Wm Wayt	1	Robt. Abbot	1
Max: Gore	7	Jno. Hancock	1	Wm Martiall	2
Jno. Abbot, Jr.	1	Wm Brittingham	5	James Atkinson	1
Isaac Glover	1	Wm Taylor	4	Wm Johnson	1
Richd. Sanders	1	Tho: Toulderbury	1	Edmd. Bowman	6
Jno. Gauslin	1	Jno. Booth	1	Wm Brown, Sr.	2
Wm Richards	1	Jno. Evans	1	Tho: Crippin	3
Ja: Truitt	1	Simon Smith	1	Roger Miles	1
Geo: Middleton	1	Wm Merrill	1	Wm Daniel	1
Hen: Bibbon	1	David Jones	1	Fran: Cooke	1
Wood: Stockley	1	Edwd. Moore	1	Ralph Justice	2
Jno. Stratton	2	Oliver Morgan	1	Jno. Blocksom	1
Cha: Colvert	1	Wm Page	1	Wm Silverthorne	1
Wm Shepherd	1	Hen: Toules	1	Peter Clavill	1
Rich: Price	1	Elias Tayler	4	Wm Willet	2
Robt. Hawley	1	Wm Blake, Sr.	3	Jno. Lawes	1
Richd. Hasting	2	Nath: Ratcliff	2	Roger Ternall	1
Jno. Custis	8	Danl Jenifer	14	Jno. Gray	1
Danl. Harwood	1	Jno. Watts	4	Rich: Hinman	3
Rich: Flowers	1	Wm Daniel	2	Wm Jerman	3
Jno. Hudson	2	Jo: Newton	3	Jo: Woodland	2
Peter Morgan	1	Jno. Prettiman	2	Wm Parker	3
Jno. Jackson	1	Jonath. Ailworth	1	Edwd. Baily	2
Geo: West	1	Nath: Tunnell	1	Rich: Bundick	2
Hen: Brooks	1	Jno. Massey	2	Ja: Forbus	1
Rich: Cooper	--	Wm Atkins	2	Jno. Ellit	1
Jo: Macknall	--	Walt: Hendrick	1	Jno. Wheeler	3
Jno. Wallop	6	James Tailer	1	Jno. Parkes	1
Hen: Rogers	2	Jno. Ferrill	1	Xopr. Thomson	2
Jno. Francisco	3	Tho: Wheeler	1	Fran: Aires	3
Alex: Gould	2	Jno. Robins	1	Wm Bunting	2
Robt. Atkinson	1	Robt. Hittchin	1	Jno. Carey	2
Jno. Wheelton	1	Garrt: Supple	1	Vinc. Langford	1
Wm Benston, Sr	2	Jacob Waggaman	1	Tho: Simson	3
Alex: Benston	2	Tho: Gillet	2	Jno. Sturgis	1
Saml. Fittiman	1	Fra: Moore	1	Rich: Hase	1
Jno. Morris	1	Geo: Ginn	1	Rich: Sturgis	1
Dennis Morris	1	Edwd. Thornton	1	Jno. Dix	3
Nich: Millichop	4	Saml. Tailer	3	Ja: Ewell, Sr.	3
Wm Lucus	1	Tho: Welburne	3	Geo: Parker	3
Geo: Hope	4	Tho: Jekin	1	Wm Langheare	1
Hen: Gibbon	1	Virga. Wood	1	Jno. Onions	1

ACCOMACK TITHABLES (Tax Lists): 1663 - 1695

Name	Tithes	Name	Tithes	Name	Tithes
Tho: Ryley	2	Cha: Leatherbury	2	Henry Dighton	1
Robt. Davis	2	Tho: Fooks	3		
Edwd. Brotherton	2	James Bonewell	3	Mr. Richd. Bally's	
		Wm Wise	1	prcincts	
Capt. Custis prcincts		Teage Andross	3	Edmd. Scarburgh	3
Walter Hargis	3	Ja: Tisaker	1	Tho: Clarke	2
Jno. Pettijohn	2	Geo: Parker	5	Jo: Clarke	1
Ed: Hitchin	1	Peter Pritchard	2	Geo: Smith	2
Rich: Carretson	2	Peter Pritchard, Jr.	1	Tho: Alom	1
Wm Dennison	2	Wm Phillips	2	Jno. Perring	2
Hen: Allin	1	Daniel Byles	1	Robt. Hutchinson	4
Rich: Nicholson	3	Perry Leatherbury	2	Hen: Read	4
Rich: Marriner	3	Jno. Wise	8	Owen Collonon	3
Wm Tilney	1	Jos: Robinson	4	Jno. Read	2
Hen: Custis	4	Robert West	2	Obed: Andrews	2
Arth: Upshor	7	Jno. Morgan	1	Simon Foscue	2
Ja: Walker, Sr.	1	Tho: Taylor, Coopr	1	Wm Andrews	1
Jno. Mellony	1	Mich: Wardell	1	John Savage	4
Garret Hitchin	1	David Nelson	2	Jno. Washbourne	4
Edwd. Burd	2	Gervas Baggaly	1	Jos: Amus	2
Jno. Willis, Jr.	1	Patrick Morgan	1	Danl. Darby	3
Wm Twyford	1	Jno. Stanton	1	Jno. Nelson	1
Wm Nock	4	Jno. Burrock	1	Tho: Nicholson	1
Hen: Chancey	2	Jno. Charles	1	Wm Littlehouse	1
Hen: Lurton	1	Jno. Alford	2	James Gray	1
Robert Taylor	1	Edwd. Johnson	1	Danl. Ograyhan	2
Wm Lingo	1	Richd. Butler	1	Wm Wale	1
Jno. Michael	3	Jno. Chandler	1	Geo: Charnock	1
Robt. Walker	2	Stevan Warrington	2	Jno. Holding	1
Jno. Revell	4	Wm Finney	1	Ja: Chapman	1
Jno. Rogers	1	Fra: Mackemy	3	Nich: Dunn	1
Tho: Francklin	1	Edmd. Tatham	3	Hen: Selman	1
Jno. Willis, Sr.	3	Cha: Scarburgh	13	At Andua - Frank,)	
Robt. Edge	1	Tully Robinson	2	negro	)1
Tho: Tailer, Shoomakr.	1	Edmd. Custis	5	And: Steward	3
Edwd. Kellam	3	Jno. Littleton	2	Robt. Watson	4
Hen: Stakes	1	Jno. Baily	5	Robt. Watson, Jr.	1
Wm Kellam	2	Wm Thoroton	1	Petr. Watson	1
Wm Burton	5	And: Stopp	1	Dormt. Sullivant	4
Jno. Welsh	1	Jno. Lewis	1	Jno. Gill	1
Saml. Beech	1	Jno. Fisher	1	Fran: Roberts	4
Nathl. Bradford	9	Alex: Nates	4	Fran: Wainhouse	4
Tho: Wilkinson	1	Arth: Donus	2	Tho: Middleton	1
Edwd. Allin	3	Jo: Hooke	1	Jno. Taylor	1
Wm Custis	5	Jno. Hickman	3	Ab: Taylor	1
Peter Burnely	1	Jo: Thorne	1	Ab: taylor, Jr.	1
		Wm Hutson	4	Rich: Niblet	1
Mr. Jo: Robinson prcincts		Robt. Jarvis	1	Tho: Burrows	1
Jno. Parker, Sr.	6	Arth: Frame	1	Wm Fletcher	2
Jno. Fenn	3	Hen: Hutton	1	Wm Alford	1
Tho: Farmbrow	2	Frans. Wharton	3	Jno. Walker	1
Alex: Harrison	2	Jno. Drumond	3	Alex: Richards	1
Rich: Cutler	1	Wm Chance	2	Arnold Harrison	2
Jno. Jenkins	3	Rich: Hill	4	Tho: Willson	2

ACCOMACK TITHABLES (Tax Lists): 1663 - 1695

Name	Tithes	Name	Tithes	Name	Tithes
Jno. Spires	1	The List of Tithables for Accomack			
Rich: Hoveington	1	County for A.D. 1691			
Robt. Munck	1				
Rich: Melton	1	Capt. Wallops prcincts.			
Jno. Milby	2	Saml. Tailer	4	Wm Glover	)
Jo: Milby	2	Henry Toules	2	at Mr. Stratton)	1
Rowld. Savage	1	Wm Arundell	1	Tho: Stokly	1
Rich: Savage	1	Wm Tailor	4	Jno. Jackson	1
Widdow Major	2	Nath: Ratcliff	2	Tho: Wheeler	1
Peter Rogers	1	Elias Tailor	4	Jno. Robins	1
Rich: Rogers	1	Wm Waight	3	John Watts	5
Tho: Bowles	1	Tho: Tounsen	1	Jonath: Owen	1
Teackle Walthom	1	Saml. Sandford	5	John Collins	1
Jno. Pratt	1	Peter Walker	3	Saml. Fittiman	1
Jno. Walthum	3	Peter Morgan	1	Jam: Tailer, Jr.	1
David Gibbons	1	John Hudson	2	Van Nelson	2
Jno. Simcock	2	Geo: West	3	Jno. Wheelton	1
Jno. Rowles	3	James Glenn	1	Robt. Atkins	1
Wm Sill	1	Will: Wright	1	Cha: Colvert	1
And: Pitts	1	Edwd. Thorneton	1	Nath: Price	1
Jno. Chace	1	Jno. Gladin	1	Hen: Brombill	1
Wm Pilcher	1	Wm Daniell	2	Simon Smith	1
Tho: Pratt	1	Nich: Millechop	3	Jno. Wheeler	1
Hen: Riden	1	James Hartly at)		Roger Miles	1
Wm Sentless	1	Martha Eyres)	1	Edw: Wright	1
Robt. Tomson	2	Wm Lucus	1	James Askew at)	
Wm Betes	1	Ralph Justice	1	Robt. Burtons)	1
Mr. Tho: Teackle	5	Att Francis Jesters)		John Bloxum	2
Geo: Hazelop	1	is Rich: Jester,)	2	Hen: Brooks	1
Wm White	3	Jr., Saml. Jester)		Robt. West	1
Rich: Bally, Jr.	1	Jona: Aleworth	1	Hen: Hubanck	1
Wm Goulden	1	Wm Shepard	1	Jno. Preteman	1
Wm Heath	1	Rich: Cooper	1	Jeremia Wood	1
Ja: Longo	1	Tho: Perry	2	Danl. Harwood	1
Jno. Lecatt	2	Jos: Stokeley	1	Jno. Hews	1
Mich: Richards	2	Wm Blake, Jr.	2	Jno. Abbot, Sr.	2
Rich: Balley	3	John Blake	1	Rich: Hinman	4
Geo: Nich: Hack	8	Dennis Morris	3	Tho: Mills	1
Geo: Johnson	4	Jos: Newton	3	Julian Martin	1
Robt. Norton	2	Wm Blake, Sr.	2	Saml. Young	2
Tim: Coe	1	Fran: Stokeley	1	Tho: Simson	3
Wm Ballard	1	John Scott	1	Garrt. Sipple	1
Julian Martin	1	John Deale	1	Hen: Sadbery	1
Jno. West, Sr.	13	James Tailer, Sr.	1	Wm Atkins	1
Rich: Meers	1	Alex: Massy, Jr.	2	Will: Parker	4
Law: Ryley	1	Alex: Johnson	1	Gabriel Watts at)	
Ja: Alexander	1	John Masse	1	Sevats	)1
Arth: Tull	1	Wm Paterson	1	Geo: Ginn	2
Tho: Tounsend	1	Tho: Toldersbee	1	Jos: Gladin	1
Peter Bootee	1	Wm Paine	1	Will: Silverthorne	2
Rich: Kellam	4	Jno. Hancok	1	John Aires, Jr.	1
Mrs. James	3	Jacob Wagaman	2	Abell Johnson	1
The totll of ye Tithbles 731				Wm Johnson	1

v. ix - p. 190

ACCOMACK TITHABLES (Tax Lists): 1663 - 1695

Coll Danl. Jenifer	14	Abraham Bancks)	1	Edwd. Hitchin	2
James Powell	1	Pocomoke)		Walter Hargis	1
Hen: Rogers	1			Tho: Tailer,Cordwr.	1
John Francisco	1	Coll Jenifers prcincts		Robt. Taylor	1
Alex: Gold	3	John Sturgis	1	Tho: Ironmonger	2
Max: Gore	5	John Hickman	2	Francis Crossly	1
David Hasard	2	Rich: Greenall,Const.	2	Widow Michael	3
James Smith	2	John Jones	1	Widow Bagwell	4
Mr. Wm Anderson	11	Wm Willet	3	Edmd. Allin,Const:	2
John Booth	3	Rich: Sanders	2	John Willis, Sr.	3
David Jones	1	Arthur Frame	1	John Willis, Jr.	1
Lues Debrear)	1	George Middleton	3	Arth: Upshor	7
at Sevats)		Wm Litchfeild	1	David Alford	1
Tho: Gillet	2	John Ellet	1	Robt. Sample	1
James Truet	1	Wm Daniel	1	Saml. Beech	1
John Arue	1	Wm Brown	1	David Griffin	1
Jno. Gray	1	James Atkinson	1	John Rodgers	2
Jno. Parka	1	Wm Jarman	4	Jno. Spires	1
James Davis	1	Geo: Parker, Sr.	2	Tho: Wilson	1
Peter Booten	1	Geo: Johnson, Sr.	3	Ed: Bird	2
Roger Ternall	2	Tim: Coe	2	Jno. Charles	1
Alex: Benston	1	Anth: Gerrard	1	Wm Nock	4
Peter Clavill	1	Edward Carter	1	Hen: Lurton	2
Hen: Gibbin	1	Francis Cook	1	Rich: Melton	1
Robt. Davis	2	Edmd. Tatham	2	Henry Chancy	2
John Wallop	7	Rich: Haze	1	Hen: Stakes	2
Tho: West	1	John Barnes	5	Widow Meares	2
Wm Benston, Sr.	2	att Mary Grotons	2	Robt. Walker	1
Edwd. Moore	2	Tho: Crippin	2	John Revell	4
John Evans	1	Wm Marshall	1	William Tilney	1
Wm Ballard	1	John Marshall	1	Hen: Custis	3
Robt. Haly	1	Edmd. Bowman	6	Rich: Kellam	4
Fra: Wharton	3	Moses Marvill	1	Edwd. Kellam	3
Tho: Nickson	1	Vincent Langford	1	Wm Kellam	2
Rich: Price	1	Jno. Cary, Sr.	3	John Burrick	1
Edwd. Broderton	2	Xtopr. Tomson	2	Andrew Steward	3
Fra: Moor	1	Joseph Woodland	1	Alex: Notes	3
John Abbot, Jr.	2	Edwd. Bayley	2	Rich: Parrimore	2
Jos: Wagnah ay Jesters	1	Joseph Thorne	1	Wm Twyford	1
Lewis Knight	3	Ja: Furbush	1	Wm Bradford	6
Nath: Tunnell	1	Tho: Jenkins	1	Wm Custis	5
Wm Page	1	Geo: Hope	3	Wm Burton	4
Will: Britingham	3	Fra: Ayres	2	Peter Burnly	1
Wm Benston, Jr.	1	Tho: Rayley	3	Jno. Onions	3
John Custis, Jolleys)		James Yewell	3	Wm Yeo	2
Neck)	9			John Cole	3
Jos: B----- "	6	Capt. Wm. Custis prcts		Morgan Lysons	1
Ja: Cuddy	1	Wm Dennison	4	Rich: Jacob	1
Wm Hudson	2	James Walker	1	Wm Bunting	2
Rich: Hastings	1	Rich: Marriner	4		
Wm Hall	1	Hen: Allin	1	Mr. Robinsons prcts.	
Mr. Tho: Welburne	4	Rich: Nickollson	1	John Drumond	5
Wm Goff added to)		Jno. Pettejohn	2	Capt. Rich: Hill	5
Peter Walker's list)	1	Rich: Garritson,Const.	1	Wm Chance	2

ACCOMACK TITHABLES (Tax Lists): 1663 - 1695

Name	Tithes	Name	Tithes	Name	Tithes
John Lewis	3	Wm Wise	1	Wm Alford	1
John Wise	7	Mr. Mekennys	3	James Chapman	1
Johannes Wise	1	Hen: Dighton	1	Tho: Williams	1
Teage Anderson	2	Nich: Hill	1	Hen: Read	2
Step: Warrington, Constable	)) 1	Mr. Rich: Bally his prcincts		Wm Mason Wm Heath	1 1
John Chandler	1			Danl. Darby	4
Wm Finney	1	Edmd. Scarburgh	4	Wm Darby	1
Tho: Webb	2	John Washbourne	4	Fran: Robins	4
Peter Pritchard	1	Hen: Selman	1	Geo: Smith	2
Wm Rawlins	1	Jno. Downing	1	Tho: Bud	7
John Baily	5	Tho: Clarke	1	Roger Kirkman	1
Patrick Morgan	1	Owen Collonon	3	Fran: Garganus	1
Henry Hutton	1	Wm Sill	2	Robt. Hutchinson	1
Jno. Richardson	1	John Nellson	2	Paul Johnson	1
Jno. Parker	3	Jos: Ames	3	John Rowles	2
Wm Parker	1	Jos: Clarke	1	Wm Betts	1
Robt. Parker	1	Wm Littlehouse	1	Dormt. Sullivant	3
John Lilliston	2	Jo: Ash	1	Peter Watson	1
Tho: Daisy	1	At James Grayes	)	Wm Goulding	1
Wm Thoroton	1	James Lory	) 1	John Perring	1
John Fisher	1	Rich: Rogers	1	John Milby	1
John Littleton	1	Jno. Read	2	Wm White	2
Coll Jno. West	12	Jno. Walthum	3	Tho: Burrows	2
Antho: West	4	Geo: Charnock	1	Robt. Munck	1
Alex: West	2	Fran: Wainhouse	3	Tho: Boules	1
Widdow Leatherbury	2	Jno. Savage	6	Rich: Jones	1
David Nellson	1	Robt. Thomson	2	Simon Foscue	2
John Jenkins	3	Cornls. Harman	2	At Mr. Littletons Franck	1
John Stainton	2	Wm Lingo	1		
John Fenn	2	Robt. Watson	4	Peter Rogers	1
And: Stop	1	Mich: Richards	1	John Chace	1
John Alford	1	John Fogo	2	Wm Pilcher	1
Tho: Fooks	3	Teackle Walthum	1	Robt. Andrews	3
Rich: Cutler	2	Arnul Harrison	2	Wm Andrews	1
Alex: Harrison	4	Geo: Nich: Hack	10	At Mr. Teackles	6
Gervas Bagaly	2	John Watts	1	John Simcock	1
Tho: Taylor, Coopr.	1	Alex: Richards	2	John Walker	2
Tho: Bushell	2	James Longo	1	Rich: Niblet	1
Tho: Farmbrow	1	Tho: Nickolson	1	Rich: Bally	1
Jo: Robinson	2	Wm Rogers	1	Rich Bally, Sr.	3
Pet: Prichard, Jr.	1	Jno. Lecatt	4		
Ja: Tisacar	1	Rowd. Savage	2	The Totll. Tithables	
Arth: Donus	2	Abraha: Taylor	1	762	
John Lawes	1	John Tailer	2		
James Bonewell	2	Tho: Middleton	1	v. ix - p. 227	
Wm Phillips	2	Geo: Hazelup	1		
Jos: Hooke	1	Robt. Watson	1		
Perry Leatherbury	2	At Widow Majors	1		
Rich: Butler	--	Joseph Milby	1		
Mr. Geo: Parker	4	Danl. Ograyhan	2		
Maj. Cha: Scarburgh	12	John Pratt	1		
Mr. Tully Robinson	2	Wm Fletcher	2		

ACCOMACK TITHABLES (Tax Lists): 1663 - 1695

The List of Tithables for A.D. 1692 belonging to Accomack County

Name	Tithes	Name	Tithes	Name	Tithes
Mr. Wm Anderson his prcts.		Lewis Knight	2	Jno. Hudson	1
James Davis	1	Julian Martino	1	Richard Jester	2
John Bloxum	2	Martin Venetson	1	James Tayler, Jr.	1
Wm Cheseman	1	James Glenn	1	James Tayler, Sr	2
Jno. Booth	1	Wm Lewis	1	Edmd. Needham	1
Tho: Jenkins	1	Wm Paine	1	Hen: Sadbury	1
Geo: Key	1	Hen: Brombill	1	Jno. Beasley	1
Jno. Newton	3	Wm Blake, Jr.	1	Wm Benston, Sr.	2
Tho: Townsend	1	John Blake	1	Alexdr. Benston	1
Jno. Custis	6	Wm Blake	4	Ralph Justice	2
Sebast: Delastius	4	Hen: Rogers	1	Jno. Jones	1
Wm Jerman	5	John Francisco	2	Wm Benston, son of	
Edward Moore	2	Jno. Robinson	1	Fran: Benston	1
George Ginn	2	Edwd. Robins	4		
Joseph Glading	1	Nathl. Tunnell	1	Mr. Burton his prcts.	
Jona. Aileworth	1	Max: Gore	6	Arthur Upshor	7
Jno. Prettiman	1	Abrah: Shepperd	1	Hen: Stakes	3
Simon Smith	2	Fran: Stockley	1	John Willis	3
Wm Page	1	Edwd. Thornton	1	John Willis, Jr.	1
Robt. Crowson	1	James Smith	1	Rich: Melton	1
Saml. Fittiman	2	Saml. Tailer	4	Wm Lingo	3
Joseph Bird	1	Tho: Stokeley	1	Edwd. Bird	2
Rich: Flowers	1	Mr. Stratton	1	Jno. Meeres	1
Dennis Morris	1	Joseph Stokeley	1	Wm Meers	1
Jno. Morris	1	Wm Lucus	1	Robt. Meers	1
Wm Tailer, Jr.	1	Nich: Millechop	4	Wm Bradford	6
Saml. Sandford	6	Alex: Gold	2	Hen: Custis	3
Seba: Delastius, Jr.	1	Robt. Atkins	1	Tho: Tayler	3
James Kude	1	Jno. Wheelton	1	Jno. Rogers	1
Wm Stripe	1	Peter Watson	2	Wm Twyford	1
John Evans	1	James Powell	1	Rich: Parramore	2
Wm Shepard	1	John Abbot	2	James Walker	1
Peter Booty	1	Hen: Gibbons	1	Robt. Couleburne	2
Jacob Wagaman	2	Walter Mackhendrick	1	Saml. Beech	1
Garrit Supple	1	Wm Wright	2	Robt. Edge	2
Wm Brittingham	4	Rich: Price	1	Hen: Allin	1
Widdow Daniels	2	Jno. Mills	1	Jno. Spires	1
David Jones	2	Elias Tailer	5	Hen: Chancey	2
Wm Paterson	1	Tho: Allen	1	Wm Nock	5
Alex: Massie	5	Tho: Foldersby	2	Hen: Lurton	2
Wm Anderson	12	Jno. Bonner	1	Tho: Willson	2
		Tho: Perrey	2	Wm Dennison	3
Capt. Wallop his prcts.		Jno. Glading	1	Robt. Taylor	1
Jno. Hues	1	Rich: Cooper	1	Jno. Mellony	1
Cha: Colvert	1	Jno. Watts	3	Morgan Lysons	1
John Wallop	6	Jno. Collins	1	Fran: Crawsey	1
Peter Morgan	1	Anth: Gerwood	1	Robt. Walker	1
Wm Tailer	4	Jno. Deane	1	Tho: Ironmonger	1
Jona. Owen	1	Peter Walker	3	Edward Hitchin	1
Rich: Hastings	1	Hen: Towles	1	Garret Hitchin	1
Wm Weight	2	Hen: Brookes	2	Walter Hargress	1
Danl. Harwood	1	George West	3	Richd. Garretson	2

ACCOMACK TITHABLES (Tax Lists): 1663 - 1695

Name	Tithes	Name	Tithes	Name	Tithes
Jno. Revell	5	Rowld. Savage	4	Jno. Chandler	1
Jno. Michael	2	Antho: West	5	Arth: Donis	1
Richd. Kellam	3	Alex: Richards	2	Tho: Webb	1
Richd. Kellam, Jr.	1	Wm Milby	1	Tho: Taylor	1
Wm Kellam	2	Saml. Hutton	1	James Bonewell	2
Edwd. Kellam	3	Robt. Hutchinson	3	Patrick Morgan	1
Jno. Tire	4	Wm Fletcher	5	Jno. Richardson	1
Wm Tilney	1	Jno. Walker	1	Wm Phiney	2
Edmd. Allin	4	Saml. Doe	1	Jno. West	11
Geo: Marriner	1	Jno. Milby	1	Robt. Parker	1
Wm Custis	6	Jo: Milby	1	Tho: Simpson	1
Wm Burton	4	James Longo	1	Mr. Mackenny	4
Robt. Scott	1	Jno. Rowles	2	Tho: Smith	1
		Fran: Garganis	1	Hen: Hutton	1
Capt. Bally his prcincts		Wm Pilcher	1	Wm Silverthorne	1
Edmd. Scarburgh	4	Joseph Clark	2	Robt. Norton	3
Mikell Richards	2	Jno. Washbourne	3	Jno. Parker, Sr.	3
Ab: Tailer, Jr.	1	Richd. Niblet	1	Tully Robinson	2
Tho: Boules	1	Fran: Wainhouse	3	Peter Turlington	1
Rich: Hoveington	1	Rich: Waters	4	Step: Warrington	1
Rich: Rogers	1	David Watson	2	Gervace Baggaley	3
Peter Rogers	1	Robt. Andrews	1	Tho: Farmbarrow	2
Robt. Munck	1	James Gray	2	John Jenkins	2
Jno. Walthum	3	Francis Roberts	4	John Fisher	3
Teackle Walthum	1	Jno. Pratt	1	Rich: Cutler	2
Alexdr. Notes	1	Geo: Smith	3	Alex: Harrison	3
Alexdr. Steward	5	Wm Golding	1	Jno. Broadhurst	3
Wm French	3	Wm Darby	1	Jno. Alford	1
Jno. Nellson	2	Jno. Perrey	1	Wm Phillips	2
Mr. Teackle	6	John Savage	6	Perrey Leatherbury	2
Robt. Watson, Sr.	3	Simon Foscue	3	Geo: Parker	4
Wm Bettes	1	Cornels: Harman	1	Johannes Wise	1
Danl. Darby	4	Robt. Watson, Jr.	2	John Lewis	1
Tho: Clarke	1	Peter Watson	1	Joseph Towser	1
Owen Collonon	3	Robt. Thompson	3	Tho: Fowkes	4
Wm Sill	2	Hen: Selman	1	Wm Rawlins	1
Hen: Read	5	James Chapman	1	Wm Wise	1
Jno. Read	1	Wm Andrews	1	Teige Anderson	1
Wm Thureton	1	Tho: Nicholson	2	James Tizacar	1
Jno. Gaylor	1	Tho: Budd	6	John Baily	4
Paul Johnson	1	Jno. Chace	1	Wm Alford	1
Jno. Lecatt	3	Rich: Bally, Jr.	1	Jno. Lawes	1
Tho: Middleton	2	Rich: Bally, Sr.	3	Robt. West	1
Tho: Williams	1	Geo: Nich: Hack	9	Alexdr. West	3
Danl. Ograyhan	2	Andrew Pitts	1	Jo: Robinson	1
Wm Wale	1			Abel Johnson	1
Wm Mason	1	Mr. Jo: Robinsons prcts		John Charles	1
Wm Littlehouse	1	John Wise, Sr.	7	John Burrock	1
Joseph Amos	1	John Littleton	1	John Fenn	1
Tho: Burrows	2	Wm Parker	1	David Nellson	1
Jno. Fogo	3	Joseph Hooke	1	Danl. Byles	1
Wm White	3	Tho: Bushell	2	Jno. Stainton	2
Arnold Harrison	1	Peter Pritchard	1	Wm Barnes	3
Rich: Jones	2	Peter Pritchard, Jr.	1	Coll Cha:Scarburgh	14

ACCOMACK TITHABLES (Tax Lists): 1663 - 1695

	Tithes		Tithes		Tithes
Tho: Welburne	3	Jno. Coe	1		
Nath: Ratcliff	2	Jeremiah Wood	2		
Rich: Johnson	1	Robt. Davis	2		
Wm Daniel	1	Coll Jenifers prcincts.			
Mr. Edmd. Custis prcincts		Geo: Parker, Sr.	4		
Edmd. Custis	5	Rich: Sturgis	1		
Rich: Sanders	1	Mrs. Cropper	2		
Vinson Langford	1	Edwd. Wright	1		
Jno. Carey, Sr.	3	James Atkinson	1		
Xopr. Thomson	2	Tho: Bonewell	1		
Jno. Ayres	2	Jos: Woodland	2		
Fran: Ayres	2	Joseph Thorne	1		
Rich: Drumond	4	Geo: Hope	2		
Jno. Lewis, Sr.	4	Rich: Bundock	3		
Fran: Cooke	1	Hugh Fullen	4		
Arthur Frame	1	Wm Dixson	1		
Rich: Greenall	2	Robt. Bayley	3		
Jno. Parkes	1	John Onyons	2		
John Sturgis	2	James Hartly	1		
Hen: Young	2	Edwd. Brotherton	1		
John Hickman	1	John Gray	1		
Wm Hudson	2	Francis Wharton	4		
Jno. Wheeler	1	John Arew	2		
Geo: Middleton	2	John Winburrow	1		
Peter Ease	1	Jeremiah Wood	1		
Tho: Ryley	3	Tho: Furbus	2		
Roger Turnell	2	Jno. Ellet	1		
Wm Willet	1	Jno. Cole	4		
Tho: Courtney	1	At Mrs. Bowman's	3		
Hen: Lamberson	1	Robt. Hawley	1		
Math Layler	1	Danl. Jenifer	13		
Edmd. Tathum	3	John Marshall	2		
Jno. Littleton	1	Wm Tucker at Capt.)			
Jno. Abbot	2	Jno. Custis)	2		
Robt. Abbot	1	At Robt. Coleburnes)			
Wm Yeow	1	on negro called			
James Ewell, Sr.	3	Jack omitted	1		
Wm Martiall	1	Wm Litchfield	1		
Edwd. Carter	1				
Wm Chance	3	v. ix - p. 258			
Tho: Mills	1				
Wm Parker	2				
Wm Bunting	2	The List of Tithbles. for Accomack County			
Jno. Mason	1	for A.D. 1693			
Tho: Nickson	2		Tithes		Tithes
Tho: Jenkins	2	James Taylor, Sr.)		Wm Shepherd	1
Rich: Hinman, Sr.	4	Wm Taylor)	3	James Tailer, Jr.	1
Wm Ballard	1	Richard Green)		David Jones	2
Xopr. Jones	1	Garrt. Supple	1	Wm Stripe	2
Geo: Johnson	1	Rich: Smalle	1	Wm Brittingham	3
Tho: Crippin	1	John Francisco	2	Hen: Toules	2
Jno. Drumond	3	Hen: Rogers	1	Jno. Boner	1
Jno. Tounsend	2	Rich: Flowers	1	Tho: Sutars	3

ACCOMACK TITHABLES (Tax Lists): 1663 - 1695

Name	Tithes	Name	Tithes	Name	Tithes
Saml. Sandford	5	Wm Mathews	1	Jno. Carey, Sr.	3
Wm Wyat	2	Nich: Millechop	4	Rich: Greenall	1
Geo: Barret	1	Wm Lucus	1	Rich: Hickman	1
Jacob Waggaman	2	Saml. Jester	1	Arthur Frame	1
Jos: Stockley	1	Robt. West	2	Jno. Hickman	1
Alex: Massy	2	Lewis Knight	3	Jno. Custis, Jr.	3
Jno. Collins	1	Morgan Lijence	1	James Glenn	1
Jno. Newton	3	Wm Tayler	5	Wm Chance	2
Wm Benston, Jr.	1	Peter Morgin	2	Tho: Ryley, Sr.	2
David Hazard	2	Jno. Prettiman	1	Jno. Arew	1
Alex: Johnson	1	Jno. Read	1	Cha: Campleshon	1
Jno. Massy	1	Geo: Ginne	2	Robt. Norton	3
Robert Attkins	1	Hen: Brooks	1	Wm Richards	1
Wm Blake	1	Jno. Scott	1	Jno. Mason	1
James Smith	1	Ed: Moore	2	Wm Silverthorne	1
Jno. Robinson	1	Jos: Glading	1	Jno. Welch	1
Saml. Taylor, Sr.	3	Peter Booty	1	Wm Shores	1
Peter Walker, Sr.	4	James Davis	1	Fran: Cooke	2
Edwd. Robins	4	Tho: Townsend	1	Edwd. Baly	1
Hen: Gibbins	--	Jno. Glading	1	Jno. Ellet	1
James Hartly	1	Cath: Bowman	2	Robt. Abbot	1
Richard Price	1	James Atkinson	2	Tho: Crippen	3
Hen: Rich	1	Danl. Jenifer	14	Hen: Lambertson	1
Jno. Wheelton	1	Wm Parker	4	Wm Johnson	1
Fran: Stockley	1	Elias Taylor	5	Simon Smith	1
Ed: Tathum	3	Wm Anderson	12	Max: Gore	6
Xopr: Thomson	2	Wm Patterson	1	Rich: Johnson	1
Coll Custis	9	Tho: Jenkins	1	Dennis Morris	1
Jno. Custis	1	Jno. Booth	1	Jno: Lewis, Jr.	3
James Cuddy	1	Jo: Bird	1	Jno. Watts, Coopr.	4
Savat: Delastatius	2	Jno. Evans	1	Jno. Nellson	2
Xopr. Bridgwater	2	Geo: Key	2	Arthur Upshur	6
John Hutson	2	Wm Stripe	1	Edward Hitchin	1
Wm Martiall	2	Xo: Chipindale	2	Garret Hitchin	2
John Daniell	1	Wm Bunting	2	Jno. Rogers	1
Jo: Woodland	3	Jno. Cole	4	Will: Nock	5
Jno. Blocksom	3	Wm Benston, Jr.	2	Hen: Lursen	3
Danl. Esham	1	Alex: Benston	1	Hen: Chance	2
Rich: Hase	1	Jno. Dyer	1	Jno. Willis	3
Rich: Hasting	1	Skinner Wallop	5	Wm Lingo	2
Fran: Wharton	1	Nath: Tunell	1	Jno. Willson	1
Tho: Mills	1	Hen: Brombill	1	Rich: Meers	1
Bowm: Littleton	3	Wm Paine	1	J. Willis, Jr.	1
Jno. Martiall	2	Danl. Blake	1	David Alford	1
Nath: Ratlif	1	Waltr. Mackhendrick	1	Jno. Meers	1
Tho: Perry	1	Jo: Blake	2	Tho: Ironmonger	1
Wm Wright	1	Jno. Watts	5	Jno. Melony	1
Jno. Blake	2	Mart: Vanelson	1	Edward Burd	2
Ed: Thornton	1	Nath: Price	1	Wm Twyford	1
Jno. Hancock	1	Jno. Owen	1	Rich: Melton	1
Jon: Aleworth	1	James Alixander	1	Tho: Taylor	2
Robt. Rennalls	1	Jno. Ayres	3	Wm Bradford	7
Jno. Onions	2	Ralph Justice	4	Wm Dennison	4
Tho: Stockly	1	Rich: Drummond	3	Clemt. Onely	1

ACCOMACK TITHABLES (Tax Lists): 1663 - 1695

Name	Tithes	Name	Tithes	Name	Tithes
Edmd. Allin, Const.	5	Jno. Fenn	2	Rowl: Savage	3
Wm Custis	6	Wm Alford	1	Jo: Ash	1
Hen: Stakes	1	Jno. Parker, Sr.	3	Robt. Hutchinson	3
Geo: Ogelby	1	Wm Parker	1	Hen: Read	4
Hen: Hill	1	Ed: Parker	1	Arnold Harrison	2
James Walker	2	Peter Pritchard, Jr.	1	Rich: Rogers	1
Hen: Custis	3	Peter Turlington	1	Peter Rogers	1
Fran: Crossey	1	Wm Finny	1	Saml. Doe	2
James Walker, Jr.	2	Jno. West	13	Wm French	2
Walter Hargis	2	Jno. Wise, Sr.	7	Cornl: Harman	1
Rich: Kellam	3	At Fra: Mackemies	3	Jno. Lecatt, Const:	1
John Revill	5	David Nelson	1	Wm Andrews	1
Wm Tinley	1	Jno. Hutten	1	Robt Andrews	1
Tho: Bagwell	7	James Tisiker	1	Roger Kirkman	1
Hen: Allin	1	Alex: West	1	Jno. Rowles	3
Ed: Kellam	4	Tho: Webb	1	Jno. Taylor	3
Jeffrey Davis	1	Robt. West	1	And: Pitt	1
Hen: Armitrading	1	Ja: Bonewell	2	Robt. Munck	1
Rich: Garretson, Con:	1	Danl. Boyles	1	Tho: Bowles	1
Jno. Michael	1	Jno. Alford	1	Rich: Hovington	1
Wm Kellam	2	Peter Pritchard	2	Wm Mason	1
Wm Wheatly	1	Jno. Broadhurst	5	Danl. Ograyhon	2
Robt. Scott	1	Tho: Bushell	2	Jno. Milby	2
Wm Burton	8	Geo: Parker, Onancock	3	Jno. Milby, Const:	1
Tho: Farmbrow	2	Ed: Scarburgh	5	Wm Milby	1
Jno. Jenkins	2	Tho: Budd	3	Abra: Talor	1
Hen: Hutton	1	Sim: Foscue	2	Wm Fletcher	3
Perry Leatherbury	3	Jno. Downing	2	Wm Sill	2
Jno. Chandler	1	Jos: Amus	3	Jno. Pratt	1
Jno. Lewis, Cordwainr.	1	Geo: Smith	4	Owen Collonon	4
Wm Rawlins	1	And: Steward	5	James Longo	1
Jos: Towser	1	Geo: Nich: Hack	8	And: Derreekson	1
Jno. Burruck	1	Fran: Wainhouse	3	At Mr. Teackles	6
Garvas Bagaly	3	Tho: Savage	1	Mich: Rickets	2
Alexdr. Harrison	3	Wm Darby	1	Jno. Walthum	3
Jno. White	1	Wm Snelon	1	Robt. Tomson	1
Jno. Charles	1	Jno. Savage	5	Wm Betts	1
Tho: Taylor	1	Hen: Selman	1	John Perry	1
Wm Barnes	4	Tho: Williams	1	Wm Goulding	1
Jno. Stanton	3	Robt. Watson, Jr.	2	Jno. Carter	2
Jno. Warrington	2	Wm Littlehouse	1	Tho: Burrows	2
Jno. Lawes	1	Rich: Jacob	1	Wm White	3
Arth: Donis	3	Rich: Jones	2	John Washbourne	3
Tho: Foulks	2	Wm Pilsher	1	Robt. Chambers	1
And: Stopp	3	David Watson	2	Jno. Chace	1
Jno. Richardson	2	James Chapman	1	At S. Littletons)	
Patrik. Morgan	1	Jos: Clarke	3	Fra: Negro)	1
Rich: Cutler	3	Tho: Watkins	1	Teackle Walthum	1
Phill: Parker	2	Tho: Nicholson	2	Jno. Walker	1
Tho: Smith	1	Danl. Darby	3	Tho: Middleton	1
Cha: Scarburgh	15	Anth: West	6	At Widow Majors)	
Jno. Bayly	4	Wm Wale	1	Saml. Hutchsons)	1
Timo: Coe	1	Arth: Roberts	6	Peter Watson	1
Wm Phillips	1	Alex: Richards	2	Jno. Simcok	1

56

ACCOMACK TITHABLES (Tax Lists): 1663 - 1695

	Tithes		Tithes		Tithes
Rich: Bally, Jr.	3	Walter Hargis	3	Martha Eyre	1
Rich: Bally, Sr.	3	Robert Norton	2	John Hudson	1
Robt. Watson, Sr.	4	John Cary	2	James Dure	1
		Wm Davis	2	John West	2
The Totall of the List		Tho: Scott	1	Geo: Johnson	1
of Tithabls. is 816		Denish Morrish	2	John Abbot, Jr.	1
v. xi - p. 40		Wm Anderson	9	Robt. Jarvis	1
		Wm Billger	1	Rich: Drumond	3
		Wm Shepard	1	Morgon Licence	1
The List of Tithables be-		Jos: Burd	1	Nich: Milechop	5
longing to Accomack County		Tho: Jenkinson	1		
for A.D. 1694		Gabrill Waters	1	Coll Custis Tithbls	
		John Booth	1	Jno. Custis, Pocomk.	1
Mr. Ed: Custis prcnts.		John Evans	1	James Cuddy	1
Edmd. Custis	6	Wm Stripes	1	Hen: Lamberson	1
Roger Miles	1	John Glading	1	John Parker, Sr.	4
Edwd. Pitt	1	Sim: Smith	1	Danl. of St. Tho:	
Tho: Simson	1	Rich: Hayes	1	Jenifer	11
Rich: Sanders	1	Lewis Knight)		Tho: Bonewell	2
Rich: Bundick	3	John Asbon)	2	Rich: Hastings	1
Ralph Justice	3	Julian Martin	1	Wm Willson	3
John Doe	2	John Wheeler	1	Jo: Woodland	3
Tho: Smith	1	Fran: Wharton	3	Vin: Langford	1
Rich: Hinman	1	Capt. John Custis	4	Jno. Cary, Jr.	1
Robt. Davis	1	Rich: Small	1	Lance: Jacques	1
Robt. Riping	1	Robt. Pitt	1	Robt. Crouson	1
Tho: Bell	1	Danl. Esom	1	Edm: Tathom	4
John Colly	1	Wm Parker	2	Saml. Young	1
Rich: Hickman	3	Tho: Mills	1	Robt. Atkins	1
Wm Willett	2	Jonat: Aleworth	1	John Wheelton	1
John Hickman	3	James Davis	1	Wm Chance	2
John Gray	1	Edwd. Thoroton	1	Rich: Hill Ayres	1
John Ayres	1	Timo: Coe	3	Jno. Littleton	1
Wm Richards	1	John Prettiman	1	John Arue	1
Fran: Ayres	1	John Abbot, Sr.	2	John Alsop	1
Finlaw Mackwilliam	1	Robt. Abbot	1	Jno. Welch	1
Wm Lichfield	1	Wm Hudson	1	Tho: Ryle, Sr.	2
Abel Johnson	1	Geo: Midleton, Sr.	3	John Hues	1
Wm Hickman	1	Tho; Welburne	4	John Baly	4
Geo: Parker, Sr.	4	John Collins	2	Wm Taylor	5
Tho: Nickson	2	Wm Marshall	1	Nathl. Tunell	1
John Parks	2	Geo: Powncy at)		Cha: Campleshon	3
Edward Brotherton	1	Mrs. Bowmans)	3	Roger Turnall	1
Rich: Storges	2	Fran: Stockly	2	Rich: Hill	1
John Lewis	3	Wm Lucus	1	Jno. Chanler	1
John Blocksome	3	Hen: Brombill	1	Jno. Drumond	4
Wm Bunting	1	Wm Whright	1	At Mary Johnson's	2
John Cole	3	Jos: Thorne	1	Wm Young	1
Tho: Crippin	3	James Atkins	2	More belonging to)	
John Elet	1	Hen: Brooks	1	Coll Custis, viz:)	4
John Onyons	1	John Jones	1	Sebas: Delastatius	2
Edward Baly	1	Samll. Jester	3	Wm Brittingham	5
James Furbush	1	Peter Morgan	2	James Cuddy	1

ACCOMACK TITHABLES (Tax Lists): 1663 - 1695

	Tithes		Tithes		Tithes
David Jones	1	John Hooton	1	Henry Gibbons	1
Geo: Key	1	John Rogers	1	Tho: Perry	2
Jo: Gladin	1	James Bonewell	2	Alex: Marcy, Sr.	2
Jno. Beaseley	1	Tho: Taylor	1	Alex: Johnson	3
Geo: Ginn	2	Tho: Smith	1	Robt. Smith	1
Edwd. Moore	2	Robt. West	1	Jos: Stoackly	2
Alex: West	2	Geo: Hooke	1	Tho: Stockly	2
Tho: Townsen	1	Wm Phillips	2	Wm Benston, Sr.	1
John Robins	1	Richd. Cuttler	3	Richd. L. Flowers	1
Ja: Tayler, Jr.	1	Gervas Bagaly	4	Coll Jno. West	12
Tho: Staneworth	1	Tho: Bushell	2	John Simcok	1
Wm Benston	1	Alex: Harrison	3	Geo: Parker	3
Jno. Newton	1	Thomas Fookes	3	Peter Pritchard	3
Jno. Mercy	2	William Lewis	1	Perry Leatherbury	1
James Ewell	2	John Lawes	3	Jno. Carter	1
Geo: Truet	1	William Barnes	4	Patrick Morgan	1
Wm Danell	1	John Richardson	1	Alex: Morgan	1
Wm Silverthorne	2	Charles Piwell	1	Wm Johnson	1
Wm German	2	John Fisher	1	John Bradhurst	4
John Bonner	1	John Lewis	1	Wm Wise	1
Arthur Frame	1	John Stanton	4	Johannes Wise	1
Jno. Mason	1	John Jenkins	2	Tho: Wadkins	1
Jacob Waggaman	3	John Burrick	1	James Tayler, Jr.	1
Alex: Gold, Sr.	3	John Collins	1	Jos: Tozer	1
Wm Waight	2	John Fenn	1	John Wise, Sr.	7
Nich: Hill	2	Wm Rawlins	1	Coll Cha: Scarburgh	
Peeter Booty	1	Peter Pritchard, Jr.	1		15
Nath: Ratcliff	1	Robt. Ardis	1		
Peter Walker	3	Rich: Butler	1	Mr. Burtons prcts.	
Fran: Wharton, Jr.	1	John Charles	1	Arth: Upshor	7
Tho: Milman	1	Tho: Webb	1	Wm Nock	7
Elias Taylor	5	Steph: Warrington	2	Hen: Lurton	2
Jo: Cottell	1	Wm Alford	1	Robt. Tayler	1
Edwd. Carter	1	Phill: Parker	3	Hen: Chancy	2
Edwd. Robins	4	John Alford	2	Edwd. Hitchin	1
Saml. Taylor	4	Arthur Donis	3	Edwd. Bird	2
John Martiall	2	Hugh Fullin	3	John Willis	3
Bowm: Littleton	3	Robt. Bayly	1	John Willis, Jr.	2
Rich: Johnson, Mollto.	1	Xopr. Tomson	3	Rich: Melton	1
David Hazard	1	Saml. Sandford	4	Tho: Tayler, Cordwrl	
John Smith	1	Wm Boggs	3	Tho: Willson	1
Fran: Cooke	1	Edwd. Parker	1	Wm Bradford	6
Jno. Watts, Sr.	1	Tully Robinson	2	Hen: Stakes	1
John Fogo	1	James Tayler, Sr.	3	Wm Parker	2
Wm Golding, Tanger	1	Tho: Suiters	3	David Alford	1
Jno. Nellson	1	Tho: Thorenberry	2	Wm Custis	6
Jno. Nellson	2	Wm Johnson, molatto	1	Edm: Allin	3
Jno. Carter	1	Saml. Fittiman	1	Jno. Revill	5
Walk. Mackhendrick	1	Wm Benston, Jr.	1	Robt. Coleburne	2
Pat Ditcher	1	Wm Finney	1	Jno. Winburrow	1
		Wm Paterson	1	George Ogleby	1
Mr. Broadhurst his prcincts				Wm Twyford	1
David Melson	1	Garret Sipple	1	Peter Burnley	1
James Tissaker	1	Tho: Gee	1	Saml. Hutchins	1

ACCOMACK TITHABLES (Tax Lists): 1663 - 1695

Name	Tithes	Name	Tithes	Name	Tithes
Evin Evaney	1	Robt. Chambers	1	Rich: Jacob	1
Thomas Bagwell	1	Fran: Wainhouse	4	Tho: Clarke	1
Saml. Beech	2	Wm Littlehouse	2	Wm Wale	1
Simon Foscue	3	Tho: Nicholson	2	At John Lecat's	1
Wm Lingo	2	Fra: Roberts	6	Peter Watson	2
John Read	3	John Watts	1	James Longo	1
John Barnes	3	John Washbourne	2	David Watson	2
Hen: Custis	3	Nich. Garganes	1	Geo: Anthony	1
Tho: Jones	2	John Walthum	3	Wm French	1
Tho: Ironmonger	1	Teackle Walthum	1	Wm Darby	1
Danl. Harwood	1	Danl. Darby	5	Alex: Richards	2
Richard Kellam	4	John Rowles, Sr.	4	Tho: Midleton	1
Rich: Garretson, Const.	3	Anth: West	6	Wm Pilcher	1
James Glenn	1	Row: Savage	3	Wm Andros	1
Jonath: Owen	1	Saml. Doe	1	Rich: Bally, Jr.	2
Hen: Toles	1	Arnold Harrison	2	Rich: Bally, Sr.	4
Henry Bagwell	1	At Widow Major's	2	Cornelius Harman	1
Henry Allin	1	Wm Sill	2	John Downing	1
Math: Laler	1	Rich: Rogers	1	Geo: Nich: Hack	8
James Walker	3	Peter Rogers	1		
William Dennison	3	John Taylor	2	The Totll of	
Fran: Crosy	1	John Walker	2	Tithbles. 817	
James Walker, Jr.	1	John Perry	2		
Edwd. Kellam	3	Rich: Jones	2	v. xi - p. 57	
Wm. Kellam	3	John Milby	1		
Hen: Armitrader	1	Micol Richards	1		
John Meares	1	Hen: Selman	1		
Jane Blakes tithbls.	2	Geo: Hinton	1		
Danl. Blake	1	At James Gray's	1		
Hen: Hill	1	Geo: Smith	3		
Max: Gore	5	Wm Fletcher	3		
Jno. Blake	2	Wm Rogers	1		
Wm Nicholson	4	Tho: Bowles	1		
Wm Tilney	1	Robt. Munck	1		
Robt. Edge	1	Rich: Hoventon	1		
Wm Burton	8	At Jos: Milby's	1		
Wm Lang	1	Wm Milby	1		
		Abra: Taylor	1		
Mr. Bally's prcincts		And: Pitts	1		
Edm Scarburgh	6	Roger Kirkman	1		
At Mr. Teackles	7	Frank, at Andua	1		
Robt. Hutchinson	2	Jno. Morgan	1		
And: Stuart	5	Jno. Pratt	1		
Jos: Clarke	3	Arth: Hill	1		
Jos: Amos	2	Tho: Bud	1		
Wm Goulden	1	Owen Collonon	2		
Robt. Watson, Jr.	2	Rich: Niblet	1		
Tho: Williams	1	Burnel Niblet	1		
Hen: Read	2	Robt. Watson, Sr.	3		
Wm Mason	1	John Savage	4		
Hen: White	1	Tho: Savage	1		
Wm White, Jr.	2	Robt. Tomson	1		
Phill: Lecatt	1	Mathias Tyson	1		
Danl. Ograhan	1	Wm Betts	1		

ACCOMACK TITHABLES (Tax Lists): 1663 - 1695

The List of Tithables belonging to Accomack County for the Yeare 1695

	Tithes		Tithes		Tithes
Capt. Thomas Welburne's prcincts		Alexdr. Massay, Sr.	2	John Francisco	3
		John Abbot	1	John Pash	1
Samuel Sandford	2	Wm Hazard	1	Wm Paterson	1
Symon Smith	1	Henry Toles	1	Henry Rogers	1
John Evans	2	David Hazard	1	John Collins	2
John Booth	2	Robt. Ripping	1	Bowm: Littleton	4
Edward Moore	2	Ralph Justice	2	Edwd. Robins	4
William Anderson	10	Elias Taylor	5	Joseph Blake	1
John Custis, Pocomk.	1	Jno. Glading	2	Elias Blake	1
James Cuddy	1	Tho: Jenkinson	1	Danl. Blake	1
John Watts	7	Joseph Bird	1	John Blake	1
Saml. Jester	2	Wm Stripes	1	Peter Walker	5
George West	2	George Green	2		
Nathl. Parkes	2	Jno. Prittiman	1	Mr. Ed: Custis prcincts	
Thomas Perry	3	William Wyat	4		
Henry Gibbons	1	Skinner Wallop	5	John West	12
Edwd. Thornton	1	John Read	2	Tho: Webb	1
Nathaniel Tunnell	1	William Lucas	1	Jno. Littleton	1
Julian Martin	1	Robt. Garvace	1	Edm: Custis	6
John Gibbons	1	Henry Symons	1	John West, Jr.	2
Maniml. Gore	6	John Barnet	1	Bennony West	1
Tho: Welburne	2	Nich: Millechop	3	Geo: Noble	1
William Taylor	4	John Robins	1	Robt. Norton	2
William Bunting	1	Rich: Flowers	1	Wm Chance	2
Alexdr. Gold, Sr.	3	Tho: Townsend	1	Rich: Cutler	2
William Wright	1	Carrt. Supple	1	Roger Davis	1
William Benston, Jr.	1	Joseph Ash	1	Abel Johnson	1
John Dyer	1	John Bloxsome	3	Arth: Frame	2
Jonath: Owen	1	Geo: Parker, Sr.	3	Wm Brittingham	5
Alexandr. West	1	Tho: Jones	2	Rich: Hastings	1
Geo: Key	1	Rich: Sturgis	1	John Parker	5
Wm Buesher	1	Benj: Robinson	6	Edwd. Parker	1
Jno. Sharpe	1	Wm Shepherd	1	Wm Boggs	3
Thoms. Conaway	1	Coll: Jno. Custis)		Danl. Nelson	1
Jno. Bonner	1	Tithbles)	4	John Hutten	1
Waltr. Mackhenry	1	Ed: Needeme	1	Wm Phillips	2
Wm Benston, Sr.	1	Rich: Green	1	George Hope	5
Alexdr. Benston	1	Lewis Knight	2	Frans Wharton	4
Wm Benston, Jr.	1	Sebast: Delastatius	2	Tho: Nixson	3
Saml. Fittiman	2	Joseph Stockley	2	Xopr. Thomson	3
Robert Shepherd	1	Tho: Stockley	1	Tho: Mills	2
Richd. Johnson	1	Fran: Stockley	1	Wm Parker	3
Owen Millyon	1	John Thomas	1	Henry Read	1
John Hues	1	James Dour	1	Tho: Scott	1
Guslin Venelson, Jr.	1	Rich: Price	1	Rich: Hickman	1
Thom: Milmon	1	Peter Booty	1	Tim: Coe	1
Jonath: Aileworth	1	Coll: Custis	4	Fran: Ares	2
Tho: Arnold	1	James Taylor, Sr.	2	Edmd. Tatham	1
Geo: Johnson	1	James Tayler	1	James Ewell	3
Wm Senlet	1	John Martiall	1	Robt. Bayly	1
Joseph Newton	2	John Morris	1	Tho: Crippin	3
Alex: Johnson	2	Dennis Morris	1	Danl. Esam	2

ACCOMACK TITHABLES (Tax Lists): 1663 - 1695

	Tithes		Tithes		Tithes
Roger Hickmon	2	Wm Daniel	1	John Barnes	3
Wm Willet	2	Tho: Smith	1	John Barnes, Jr.	1
John Hickman	1	Wm Silverthorne	2	Geo: Truit	1
Tho: Bonewell	3	John Mason	1	Tho: Thornbury	2
Rich: Sanders	1	Finla Mackwilliam	1	Roger Miles	2
John Baly	4	John Doe	1	John Wheeler	1
Rich: Drumond	3	John Welch	1	John Onions	2
John Lewis	4	John Cole	1	Isaac Glover	1
Rich: Hinman	1	Edward Richards	1	Robt. Atkins	2
John Hinman	1	Wm Jerman	3	John Wheelton	1
Jos: Woodland	2	Peter Pritchard	2	Tho: Allen	1
Wm Lewis	2	Robt. Walker	1	Jacob Waggaman	3
Arnell Harrison	2	Danl. of St. Tho:		Wm Yeo	1
Perry Leatherbury	3	Jenifer	7	Robt. Cole	1
Rich: Bundick	4			Math: Layler	1
Hend: Johnson	1	Mr. Burton's prcincts		Hugh: Fulling	2
Wm Hickman	2	Edwd. Bird	2	Walt: Harguis	2
Edmd. Baly	2	Fowkes Davis	1	Tho: Fooks	3
Ja: Ewell, Sr.	3	Hen: Lursen	2	John Revel	6
Robt. Abbit	1	James Leary	1	Jno. Michael	1
Wm Abbit	2	James Collins	1	Ed: Bagwell, Ind:	1
Tho: Rily	3	Jarret Hitchins	1	Wm Custis	7
At Cath: Bowman's	3	John Willis	3	James Walker	2
John Lillyston	1	Arth: Upshur	7	John Fenn	1
John Ginkins	3	Wm Dennison	4	Wm Mason	1
John Drumond	4	At Ed: Allin, Const:	1	Wm Nicholson	2
James Tusicur	1	Tho: Ironmonger	1	David Alford	1
Arthr. Donis	1	Fran: Croston	1	Tho: Lay	1
John Carey, Sr.	1	John Willis, Jr.	2	Petr. Burnely	1
Jno. Carey, Jr.	1	Wm Twyford	1	Hen: Stakes	2
Lance Lajoquith	1	Wm Nock	8	Edwd. Kellam	3
Geo: Midleton	1	Henry Chance	2	Wm Kellam	1
Jeremiah Carey	4	Robt. Tayler	1	Robt. Coleburne	2
Edwd. Burman	1	Saml. Beech	2	John Rogers	2
Wm Leachfield	1	Rich: Melton	1	Tho: Bagwell	2
Rich: Hill Airs	1	Wm Lingo	2	Wm Tilney	1
James Gray	1	Rich: Garretson		John West at John)	
Jos: Thorne	1	Constble.	3	Abbots)1	
John Arue	1	Edwd. Hitchins	1	Robt. West	1
Tully Robinson	3	Hen: Armtrading	1	Morgan Lissons	1
Garvis Baggaly	3	Tho: Smith	1	Geo: Ogleby	1
Wm Hutson	2	Tho: Taylor, Cordwr.	1	Wm Bradford	5
Robt. Davis	2	Tho: Taylor, Cooper	1	Hen: Allin	1
Hen: Lambertson	1	John Charles	1	Hen: Hill	1
Edwd. Bally	1	John Chace	1	Morris Johnson	1
John Parks	2	Tho: Willson	2	Wm Burton	8
Charles Campleshan	2	Hen: Bagwell	2	Tho: Bell	1
Tho: Simson	1	Robt. Edge	1	Nich: Hill	2
Johan Wise	2	Wm Parker	1	Hen: Custis	3
John Wise, Sr.	7	John Simcok	1	Jno. Brodhurst	5
Rich: Hill	1	John Meers	1		
Jno. Ayre	2	John Downing	1	Coll Scarburghs	
Robt. Pitt	1	Wm Meers	1	prcincts	
Rich: Roborto	1	Rich: Kellam	3	Robt. West	3

ACCOMACK TITHABLES (Tax Lists): 1663 - 1695

Name	Tithes	Name	Tithes	Name	Tithes
Rich Butler	1	Fra: Wainhouse	3	Wm Pilcher	1
John Fisher	1	Peter Watson	2	Rich: Hoveington	1
John Lewis	1	Hen: Selman	1	Tho: Bowles	1
Peter Pritchet	1	Danl. Darby	5	Robt. Munck	1
John Chandler	1	Wm Darby	1	Geo: Heuton	1
John Richardson	1	Geo: Anthony	1	Rich: Bally, Jr.	2
Jos: Hooke	1	Wm Wale	2	Arnol Harrison	1
Tho: Bushell	2	Geo: Smith	2	Tho: Williams	1
Phil: Parker	1	Jno. Savage	4	Rich: Bally, Sr.	3
Margret Seaward	1	Tho: Savage	1	Tho: Wadkins	1
John Lawes	1	Mical Rickards	1	Geo: Nich: Hack	5
Andrew Stop	1	Tho: Taylor	1		
James Bonewell	2	Rich: Rogers	1	The Total of Tithbls	
John Alford	1	Peter Rogers	1	in Accomk. County	
Wm Alford	1	Wm White, Jr.	1	797	
Wm Johnson	1	Cha: White	1		
Wm Finne	2	Alex: Richards	2	v. xi - p. 99	
John Morgan	1	Jno. Taylor	1		
Wm Barnes	3	Hen: Rideing	1		
John Warrington	2	Jno. Rowles	5		
John Burrock	2	Anth: West	8		
Patrick Morgan	1	Robt. Watson, Jr.	1		
John Ellet	1	Robt. Thomson	2		
Wm Wise	1	David Watson	1		
Cha: Scarburgh	14	Owen Collonon	3		
Charles Pywell	1	Wm Sill	2		
Geo: Parker	4	Simon Foscue	3		
		Cornels. Harman	1		
Majr. Bally his prcts		Mathias Tison	1		
Edmd. Scarburgh	3	Wm Betts	1		
Robt. Watson	3	And: Stewart	5		
Robt. Chambers	2	John Washbourne	1		
Tho: Nicholson	2	Tho: Teackle	6		
John Read, Sr.	2	James Longo	1		
Tho: Clarke	2	Rich: Niblet	1		
James Chapman	1	Burnall Niblet	1		
Roger Kirkman	1	Jos: Clarke	2		
Robt. Hutchinson	2	Wm French	3		
Jno. Walker	2	Tho: Budd	2		
Teackle Walthum	2	Tho: Midleton	1		
Jno. Pratt	1	James Gray	1		
Tho: Pratt	1	J: Sheppard	1		
Wm Milby	1	Wm Littlehouse	2		
Frans: Roberts	5	Jos: Amus	2		
Arthur Roberts	1	Danl. Ograyhan	1		
Nic: Garganis	1	Abra: Taylor	1		
Henry Eburn	1	Rich: Jones	1		
Wm Fletcher	3	Rowld. Savage	3		
Arth: Hill	1	Phil: Lecat	1		
John Walthum	2	John Lecat, Sr.	1		
John Perry	1	Wm Andrus	1		
Wm Goulden	1	At Andue, Frank			
Jno. Milby	1	negro	1		
Wm Major	1	Wm Andrews	1		

INDEX

An asterisk (*) indicates that the same name appears on the page more than once.

ABBOT(Abbit, Abut) 18, 19, 21, 23, 24, 27, 29, 32, 34, 36, 39, 41, 42, *45, *47, 49, 50, 52, *54, 55, *57, 60, *61
Abchurch 28
Able (Abell) 4,6, 8, 9, 11
Aborne (see Ebourne)
Abram (Abraham) 2, 13
Addison (adison, Addyson) 1, 2, *3, 4, 6, 7, 9, 10, 13, 15, 17, 19, 21, 24, 25, 28, 30, 43
Ailworth (Ayleworth, Alworth, Aleworth, Aillworth, Aileworth) 1, 2, 3, 6, 13, 16, 18, 19, 22, 23, 125, 27, 29, 31, 42, 45, 47, 49, 52, 55, 57, 60
Alby 17
Alexander (Allixander - see"Garganus p. 13) 40, 49, 55
Alford (Alfred) 2, 38, 41, 43, 44, *46, *48, 50, *51, *53, 55 *56, *58, 61, 62
Allson 44
Allen (Allin, Allum, Allom) 15, 17, 18, 21, 24, 25, 28, *29, 31, *33, 37, 38, *40, 41, *43, *45, 46, *48, *50,*52, 53, *56, 58, 59, *61
Alligood (Allygood) *3, 5, 6
Alore 12
Alsop 57
Ames (Amos, Amus) 16, 32, 34, 36, 39, 41, 43, 46, 48, 51, 53, 56, 59, 62
Anaughton (see Onoughton &c.)
Andros (Andross, Andrus) 27, 30, 34, 39, 42, 44, 48, 59, 62
Andrews (Andrewes) 1, 2, 4, 5, 14, 17, 34, 36, 38, 41, *43, *46, *48, 51, *53, *56, 62
Anderson (Andrewson) 2, 3, 5, *6, *8, *10, *12, 14, 17, 18, 19, *21, *24, 25, 26, 28, 29, 31, 32, 33, 35, 36, 38, 42, 45, 46, 47, 50, 51, *52, 53, 55, 57, 60
Anthony 24, 31, 34, 36, 38, 41, 59, 62
Ardis 58
Arew (arue, Aierew, Rew, Rou) 5, *8, 10, 12, 14, 18, 19, 22, 23, 26,
29, 32, 33, 36, 39, 41, 42, 50, 54, 55, 57, 61
Armitrader (Armitrading) 56, 59, 61
Armstrong (Armestrong) 18, 31
Arnold 60
Arundell 49
Asbon 57
Ash 51, 56, 60
Ashby 21
Askew 49
Atkins (Attkins) 2, 11, 14, 16, 19, 25, 28, 31, *33, 35, *37, *40, *42, *44, 47, *49, 52, 55, *57
Atkinson (Atkison, Adkinson) 1, 5, 9, 10, 12, 13, *14, 19, *20, 21, 22, 23, 27, 31, 32, 35, 45, *47, 50, 54, 55
Atteage 17
Ayres (see Eyres &c.)

BACKE 16
Baker 13
Bagwell 5, 6, *8, 9, *11, *13, *15, *17, *18, *21, *23, *25, 27, 28, *29, *31, *33, *36, *38, 40, 43, 45, 50, 56, *59, *61
Baggaly (Baggaley, Bagaly) 48, 51, 53, 56, 58, 61
Ballard 41, 43, 49, 50, 54
Ball 1, 2, 3, 4
Banton 41
Bancks 50
Barker (Berker) 17, 20, 24, *25, *27, *30, 32, 44, 46
Barks (Barke) 17, 19, 26
Barnes (Barns) 3, 4, 12, 13, 19, 22, 23, 24, 25, 27, 29, 31, 33, 35, 38, 41, 46, 50, 53, 56, 58, 59, 61, 62
Barlyman 34
Barnick 32
Barnet (Barnett) 2, 3, 7, 9, 10, 13, *14, 15, 16, *20, *21, 25, 28, 30, *32, 34, 60
Barter 6
Barton 7, 9, 10, 11, 13, *15, 17, 20, 38, 45

INDEX

Barret (Barrit, Barrick, Barrat) 16, 19, 33, 37, 39, 40, 55
Basnet (Bassnet, Besnet) 23, 25, 27, 29, 33
Basent (Besent, Bessent, Besant) 19, 22, 23, 25, 27
Batson (Battson, Bateson, Batteson) 30, 32, 33, 35
Batta 16
Baugh 33
Bayly (Bayley, Bally, Baylie) 1, 2, *4, 5, *6, 8, 9, 10, 12, 16, 20, 21, 22, 24, 26, 27, 28, 29, *30, *32, 33, *34, 35, *36, 37, 38, *39, 41, *42, *43, 45, *46, 47, *48, *49, 50, *51, *53, 54, 55, 56, 57, 58, *59, 60, *61, *62
Beasly (Beasley, Beaseley, Besly, Beesly) 23, 26, 29, 31, 35, 40, 45, 52, 58
Beech (Beetch) 13, 15, 18, 22, 23, 25, 27, 29, 31, 33, 38, 40, 43, 45, 48, 50, 52, 59, 61
Belcher 14
Bele 16
Bell 1, 2, 3, 4, 7, 9, 11, 13, 15, 17 *20, 57, 61
Belley 33
Benthall 1, 6, 9, 16
Benston (Benstone) *1, 2, *3, *4, *6, 7, *8, *10, 13, 15, 16, 18, *19, 22, 23, *26, 27, 29, 31, 35, 37, *40, *42, *47, *50, *52, *55, *58, *60
Bence (Bens, Bents, Bencha) 13, 16, 19, 26, 27, 28, 31, *37, 40
Best 22, *25
Betty 26
Betts (Bets, Bettes, Betes) 13, 22, 23, 31, 34, 36, 41, 43, 46, 49, 51, 53, 56, 59, 62
Betner (Bettnor) 36, 38
Billger 57
Bird (Burd) 16, 20, 21, 24, 28, 29, 31, 33, 38, 40, 43, 45, 48, 50 *52, *55, 57, 58, 60, 61
Bishop (Bishopp, Bushop) 1, 3, 4, 5, *7, 18, 21
Black 18
Blacklock 18
Blades (Blaids) 7, 27

Blake (Blacke) 1, 2, 3, 5, 6, 8, 11, 12, 15, 18, 19, *22, 26, 27, 28, *29, 31, 32, 33, 34, 35, 36, 37, 39, *40, 41, *42, 43, *44, 45, 47, *49, *52, *55, *59, *60
Bloyes 1
Bloxom (Bloxam, Bloxum, Blocksom, Blocksum) 13, 16, 18, 22, 23, 25, 27, 29, 32, 33, 35, 37, 40, 42, 45, 47, 49, 52, 55, 57, 60
Boate (Boot) 5, 6, 7, 9 *10, 12
Boggs 58, 60
Bonwell (Bonewell) *2, 4, 5, 17, 24, 28, 30, 32, 36, 39, 42, 44, 46, 48, 51, 53, 54, 56, 57, 58, 61, 62
Bonner (Boner) 40, 52, 54, 58, 60
Bootie (Bootee, Booty, Booten) 35, 38, 42, 44, 49, 50, 52, 55, 58, 60
Booth 9, 13, 15, 17, 19, 20, 21, 22, 23, *24, 25, *27, 28, 31, 33, 45, 47, 50, 52, 55, 57, 60
Bowles (Boules) 6, 7, 9, 10, 12, 40, 49, 51, 53, 56, 59, 62
Bowen (Bowan, Booin, Boyn) 6, 8, 10, 12, 15, 18, 19, 22, 23
Bowman 1, *2, 4, 5, 6, 8, 9, *11, *12, 15, 17, 18, *19, 22, 23, 26, 27, *29, *31, *33, 35, *38, 41, *45, 47, 50, 54, 55, 57, 61
Boyles 56
Branchly 5
Brakes 16
Bracy (Brace, Brase) 1, 2, 3, 4, 6, 8, 13, 16, 18
Bramble 17
Bradford 1, 2, 3, 4, 5, 6, 8, 9, 10, 13, 14, 15, 17, 18, 22, 23, 26, 27, 29, 31, 33, 36, 38, 40, 42, 43, 45, 48, 50, 52, 55, 58, 61
Breton 28
Brickhouse (Brighouse) 1, 2, 3, 4, 5, 6, 7, 9, 11, 13, 15, 17, 20
Brickill 27
Bridge 21
Bridgewater 55
Briggs 23, 27, 29, 38
Brittingham (Brittenham, Brightingham, Brighingham) 11, 12, 16, 18, 19, 22, 23, 26, 27, 29, 31, 33, 35, 38, 40, 42, 45, 47, 50, 52, 54, 57, 60

64

INDEX

Broadhurst (Bradhurst, Brodhurst) 53, 56, *58
Brombill (Bromevill) 31, 37, 42, 44, 49, 52, 55, 57
Broughton (Broton, Browton) 24, 25, 30, 32
Browne (Brown) *1, *2, *3, *4, *5, *6, 7, *9, *10, 11, 12, *13, *14, 15, *17, *18, 19, 20, 21, 22, *23, 24, *26, 27, *29, 31, 33, 35, 38, 41, 43, 45, 47, 50
Brotherton (Broderton, Breaderton) 13, 18, 19, 22, 23, 26, 27, 30, 32, 36, 40, 42, 45, 48, 50, 54, 57
Brooks (Brookes, Brouxe, Brocks) 1, 2, 3, 4, 5, 6, 7, 9, 10, 13, 18, 19, 22, 23, 25, 27, 29, *35, 44, 49, 52, 55, 57
Bruce 10
Buck 22
Buckland 1, 3, 5, 6, 7, 9
Bucle 5
Budd (Bud) 51, 53, 56, 59, 62
Buesher 60
Bull 19, 31, 33, 35, 37
Bundick (Bunduck) 2, 4, 5, 6, *8, 11, 12, 15, *18, *19, *22, *23, *25, 27, 29, 31, 33, 35, 38, 40, 42, 45, 47, 54, 57, 61
Bunting (Bunton) 25, 27, 29, 32, 34, 36, 38, 41, 43, 45, 47, 50, 54, 55, 57, 60
Burnely 48, 50, 58, 61
Burman 61
Burton (Burtne) 5, 6, 8, 9, 11, 13, 15, 17, 18, 19, 21, 22, *23, 24, 25, *27, *29, 31, 32, *33, 34, *35, 38, *40, 41, 42, 43, 45, 47, 48, 49, 50, 52, 53, 56, 58, 59, *61
Burch 5, 13, 15
Burke (Burk) 43, 45
Burt *7, 11, 17
Burrows (Burrowes) 19, 21, 23, 29, 31, 43, 46, 48, 51, 53, 56
Burrick (Burrock, Burruck) 35, 44, 46, 48, 50, 53, 56, 58, 62
Bushell (Buchell) 9, 20, 25, 30, 32, 34, 36, 38, 41, 44, 51, 53, 56, 58, 62
Butler 46, 48, 51, 58, 62
Buton 43
Byles 17, 20, 39, 44, 46, 48, 53

CALVERT (Colvert) 1, 2, 3, 4, 5, 6, *8, 10, 18, 19, 21, 24, 25, 27, 45, 47, 49, 52

Camell 1, 7, 10, 13, 15, 21, 24, 27, 30, 31, 33, 38, 40
Campleshon (Campleshan) 55, 57, 61
Cannon 16
Canutas (See Bence)
Card (Cord) 11, 13
Carew 5
Carter, 7, *12, *14, 17, *18, 19, 21, 24, 26, 37, 50, 54, 56, *58
Cartee 10, 42
Cartwraight 39
Cary (Carey, Carie) 6, 8, 10, 13, 16, 18, 23, 26, 27, 29, 32, 34, 39, 41, 43, 45, 47, 50, 54, 55, *57, *61
Carrell 1, 2, 3
Cayle 33
Chancy (Chancee, Chancey, Chance) 8, 9, 13, 15, 18, 21, 23, 24, 27, 29, 31, 33, 35, 38, 40, 43, 45, *48, *50, 52, 54, *55, 57, 58, 61
Chancell 22
Chapwell 19
Charnock 14, 16, 20, 21, 24, 26, 28, 30, 32, 34, 38, 41, 43, 46, 48, 51
Chandler (Chanler) 32, 36, 39, 42, 44, 46, 48, 51, 53, 56, 57, 62
Chambers 28, 56, 59, 62
Chase (Chace) 1, 2, 3, 4, 5, 6, 7, 9, 10, 12, 14, 20, 21, 24, 25, 28, 30, *32, *34, 36, 38, 41, 43, 46, 49, 51, 53, 56, 61
Charlton 1, 2, 4, 8, 9, 10, 12, 14, 16, 20, 21
Charles 30, 38, 41, 43, 45, 48, 50, 53, 56, 58, 61
Chapman 38, 41, 43, 46, 48, 51, 53, 56, 62
Cheseman 52
Chippington 42
Chippendale (Chipindale) 44, 55
Churchill 12
Clarke (Clark, Clerk) *12, 14, 16, 19, 21, *24, *25, *26, 28, *30, *31, *33, 34, 36, 38, *41, 44, 46, 48, *51, *53, 56, *59, *62
Clauson 9
Clavill (Clavell, Clavel, Clovell, Clevel, Claver) 7, 9, 13, 16, 18, 19, 22, 25, 27, 29, 34, 36, 39, 40, 43, 45, 47, 50
Cleverdon 24, 26, 27, 32
Clifton 18, 19, 22, 23
Cmichael 38
Coare (Core) 11, 13, 15, 20
Cobb (Cob) 1, 5, 13, 17, 25, 28, 30, 33, 36, *38, 40, 41

INDEX

Coe 1, 2, 3, 4, 5, 6, *8, 10, 13, 16, 18, 19, 22, 26, 28, 29, 32, 34, 37, 39, 41, 43, 45, 49, 50, 54, 56, 57, 60
Cole (Coale) 12, 14, 16, 20, 22, 23, 25, 28, 29, 31, 33, 38, 40, 43, 45, 47, 50, 54, 55, 57, *61
Coleburne 52, 54, 58, 61
Collen 9
Colly 57
Collins 11, 22, *26, 31, 33, *37, 40, 42, 47, 49, 52, 55, 57, 58, 60, 61
Collony (Collona, Collonon, Collen, Collowell, Collonell, Collenon, Ocolnon) 1, 2, 3, *4, 6, 9, 10, 12, 14, 16, 19, 21, 24, 26, 28, 30, 32, 34, 36, 38, 41, 43, 46, 48, 51, 53, 56, 59, 62
Comwell 3, 4, 5
Consalues (see Gonsaloes)
Conway (Conaway) 42, 60
Conners 25
Cooke (Cook) 9, 10, 12, 15, *16, 18, 27, 31, 33, 41, 43, 46, 47, 50, 54, 55, 58
Cooper 37, 40, 42, 46, 47, 49, 52
Cope (Coope, Coop, Copes) 2, 3, 5, 7, 9, 11, 13, 15, 17, 20
Cornelison 17
Corr 17
Correne 3
Coslie 11
Costin (Costen) 13, 18
Cottell 58
Courtney 54
Cowen 12
Cox 2, 3
Crawsey (Crossey, Crosy) 52, 56, 59
Craige 31
Crabtree 11
Crichill 18
Crippen (Crippin, Cripping, Cripen) 31, 33, 35, 38, 41, 42 45, 47, 50, 54, 55, 57, 60
Crowson (Crouson) 52, 57
Cross 1
Crossly 50
Croston 45, 61
Cropper (Cropier) 4, 7, 9, 10, 12, 15, 16, 20, 31, 54
Crump *1, 2
Cuddy (Cudde) 42, 50, 55, 57, 60
Culpeper 14
Custis 3, 4, 5, 6, *8, *13, *15, 17, *18, 22, 23, 24, 25, 27, 28, *29, *31, *33, 35, 36, *38, *40, 42, *43, *45, 47, *48, *50, *52, 53,
*54, *55, *56, *57, 58, 59, *60, *61
Cutler (Cuttler) 13, 14, 17, 19, 21, 24, 25, 27, 30, 32, 34, 36, 39, 42, 44, 46, 48, 51, 53, 56, 58, 60
Cutchkill 16
Cutting (Cuttin, Cutten) 2, *7, 8, 9, 11, 13, 14, 15, 17, 20

DAISY 51
Dale 6, 12
Daniel (Daniell, Daniels, Danell) 17, 22, 23, 25, 27, 29, *31, 33, 35, 37, 40, 42, 43, *45, *47, 49, 50, 52, 54, 55, 58, 61
Dangerfield 26
Darby (Derby) *2, 4, 5, 6, 7, 9, 10, 12, 15, 16, 20, 21, 23, 25, 28, 30, 32, 34, 36, 38, 41, 43, 46, 48, 51, *53, *56, *59, *62
Davis 1, 12, 13, 16, *18, 19, 22, *23, 26, 27, 28, 29, 30, *32, 33, *35, 37, 38, 39, *40, 41, 42, 44, *45, 46, 47, 48, *50, 52, 54, 55, 56, *57, 60, *61
Deane 27, 29, 31, 33, 52
Deale 49
Debrear 50
Delastatious (Delastaties, Delastatius, Delastacios, Delestase) 10, 14, 23, 26, 27, 29, 31, 33, 35, 37, 42, *52, 55, 57, 60
Dent 24, 28
Dennis (Denis) 3, 4, 5, 6, *8, 10, 12, 16, 18, 22, 23, 27, 29, 32, 33, 35, 37, 40, 42
Dennison (Denison) 32, 34, 41, 48, 50, 52, 55, 59, 61
Denwood 1, 2, 3
Derreekson 56
Devenish 20
Dewey (Dewy, Dewe, Duy, Due) 7, 10, 13, 15, 17, 20, 21, 23, 25, 30, 31, 37, 38, 41
Dewells 20
Die (Dyee) 1, 2, 14
Dighton 39, 48, 51
Dine (Dyne) 2, 4, 5, 17, 19
Ditcher 58
Dix 5, 12, 16, 18, 19, 22, 23, 24, 27, 29, 31, 33, 35, 38, 40, 47
Dixson 54

INDEX

Dolby (Dolbye, Dalby) 2, 3, 4, 7, 9, *11, *13, 15, *17, 20, 33
Donis (Donus) 28, 42, 44, 46, 48, 51, 53, 56, 58, 61
Dorton 16
Doss 23
Doughty 7
Dow (Doe) 1, 2, *3, 5, *7, 9, 10, 13, 15, 17, 22, 23, 25, 26, 28, 30, 31, 34, 37, 38, 39, *41, 47, 53, 56, 57, 59, 60
Dowell 4, 7, 43
Downing 51, 56, 59, 61
Drumon (Drumond) 2, 3, 4, 5, 6, *8, 10, 12, 14, 18, 19, 22, 23, 24, 27, 29, 32, 34, 36, 39, 41, *43, 45, 48, 50, *54, 55, *57, 61
Dugins 19
Dunbar 25, 28
Dungwood 15
Dungworth 12
Dunn (Dun) 26, 27, 28, 30, 32, 34, 36, 38, 41, 43, 46, 48
Dunston 3
Dure (Dour) 57, 60
Durmon 1
Dyer 33, 55, 60

EASE 54
Ebourne (Aborne, Eburn) 3, *4, 6, 7, 9, 62
Edge 27, 30, 31, 33, 35, 40, 43, 48, 52, 59, 61
Edwards 1, 2, 3, 4, 20, 23, 33, 45
Ellis 33
Ellet (Ellit, Elet) 43, 45, 47, 50, 54, 55, 57, 62
Elvin, 12
Emmet 21
Esham (Essam, Esom, Esam, Ecion, Etion, Etiam) 2, 3, 4, 5, 6, 7, 9, 11, 13, 15, 17, 20, 55, 57, 60
Evaney 59
Evans (Evan, Evens, Evins) 3, *7, 11, 13, *16, 18, 19, 22, *23, 25, 26, 28, 30, 31, 33, 34, 35, 36, 38, 42, 44, 47, 50, 52, 55, 57, 60
Ewell (Euels, Uell) 6, 8, 9, 10, 13, 15, 17, 18, 21, 24, 26, 27, 34, 36, 39, 42, 43, 45, 47, 50
Eyres (Eyre, Ayres, Ayre, Ares, Airs) 1, 2, 4, *8, 10, 12, 14, 18, 22, 23, 26, 27, 29, 31, 33, 34, 35, 36, 37, 39, 41, 42, 43, 45, 47, *49, 50, *54, 55, *57, 60, *61

FAIRFAX 42
Faree 19
Farmbrugh (Farmbrow, Farmbarrow) 46, 48, 51, 53, 55, 56
Farnbery 42
Farrell (Ferrell, Ferrill) 37, 40, 44, 47
Farrington 31, 35, 37
Fatherly 18
Fawsett (Fawset, Fauset) 1, 2, 3, 4, 5, 6, 7, 9, 10, 12, 15, 16, 21, 48
Feild 17
Felton 31
Fenn (Fen) 9, 10, 13, 14, 17, 18, 21, 24, 26, 28, 29, 32, 34, 36, 39, 41, 44, 45, 48, 51, 53, 56, 58, 61, 62
Filby (see Phillby)
Finney (Finny, Finne, Finnee, Finah, Phiney) 1, 2, 3, 4, 6, *8, 10, 35, 39, 48, 51, 56, 58
Fisher 1, 2, 3, 4, 5, 6, 7, 9, 11, 13, 15, 17, 20, 25, 28, 31, 37, 39, 42, 44, 46, 48, 51, 53, 58, 62
Fittiman 38, 42, 47, 49, 52, 58, 60
Fitzgerrald (Fitzgarrell) 34, 36, 39
Fleare 26
Fleming 4
Fletcher 14, 16, 21, 24, 25, 28, 30, 32, 34, 36, 38, 41, 43, 46, 48, 51, 53, 56, 59, 62
Floyd 44
Flowers (Flower, Floues) 29, 31, 35, 37, 40, 42, 44, 47, 52, 54, 58, 60
Fogo 51, 53, 58
Foldersby 52
Fookes (Fowkes, Foulks, Fowke, Fooke, Fooks, Focks) 1, *2, 3, *4, *5, *6, 7, 8, *9, *10, *12, 13, *14, 15, 17, 18, 19, *21, 22, 23, 24, *25, 27, 28, *30, *32, 34, *36, 39, 42, 44, 46, 51, 55, 56, 58, 61
Forbes (Forbus) 21, 40, 45, 47
Forme 23
Forse 6
Foscue (Foscew, Foskue, Foskew) 20, 21, 26, 30, 31, 36, 38, 41, 44, 46, 48, 51, 53, 56, 59, 62

INDEX

Foster 15, 17, 20, 25, 28, 32, *33, 34
Fox 28
Foxcroft 6, 7, 9, 11
Frame 12, 18, 19, 22, 23, 25, 27, 29, 32, 34, 36, 39, 41, 42, 45, 48, 50, 54, 55, 58, 60
Francis 41, 44
Francisco 12, 16, 18, 19, 22, 23, 25, 27, 28, 31, 33, 35, 37, 40, 42, 44, 47, 50, 52, 54, 60
Franklin (Frankling, Francklin) 11, 13, 15, 16, 17, 18, 21, 22, *23, *25, 27, 29, 31, 33, 40, 43, 45, 48
Freeman 13, 15, 16, 17, 23, 25, 27
French 53, 56, 59, 62
Frenchman 20
Fullen (Fullin, Fulling) 54, 58, 61
Furbush (Furbus) 38, 42, 50, 54, 57
Furs 42, 43

GALL 31, 39, 41
Galloe 7
Garganis (see Alexander p. 13)
Garganus, Garganes 18, 51, 53, 59, 62
Garretson (Garritson, Garrison, Garrittson) 15, 17, 20, 21, 25, 28, 29, 31, 33, 35, 38, 40, 43, 45, 48, 50, 52, 56, 59, 61
Garvace (see Jarvis)
Gaul (Gall) 18
Gee 58
Genner 35
German-Germane (see Jarman &c.)
Gerrard 47, 50
Gerwood 52
Gery 12
Gesture 40
Gibbons (Gibons, Gibbin, Gibbins) 6, 8, 12, 17, 20, 21, 24, 25, *34, *36, 38, 39, 41, 42, 43, 44, *46, *47, 49, 50, 52, 55, 58, *60
Gill 48
Gillet (Gillit, Gilliet, Gilliot, Gillett, Jillit) 5, 6, *8, 11, 12, 42, 44, 47, 50
Gillrean 27
Gilson (Gelson, Gellson) 31, 33, 39, 45, 47
Ginee 15

Ginkins (see Jenkins)
Ginn (Gin, Ginne) 12, 15, 16, 20, 21, 24, 25, 28, 30, 32, 34, 36, 39, 41, 42, 45, 47, 49, 52, 55, 58
Gittins (Gittings, Githing) 5, *7, 11, 13, 15, 17
Glading (Gladding, Gladin) 4, 5, 6, 7, 9, 10, 12, 16, 18, 19, 22, 23, 25, 27, 29, 31, 34, 35, 37, 42, 47, *49, *52, *55, 57, 58, 60
Gladwin 40
Glenn 49, 52, 55, 59
Glew (Glue) 13, 15, 17, 20, 25, 27, 30
Glover 23, 42, 45, 47, 49, 61
Goff 50
Gonsaloes (Gonsaloos, Gonsolvoe, Consalues) 13, 14, 17, 19
Goodman 14, 20
Gordin (Gording, Gordian, Garding) 1, 9, 13, *15, 20, 21
Goring (Goreing) 2, *3, 5, 6, 10, 17
Goslin (Gozoling, Gauslin, Goslee) 9, 10, 12, 47
Gothogon (Gogahan, Gohogon) 39, 41, 43
Gould (Gold, Goold) 44, 47, 50, 52, 58, 60
Goulding (Gouldin, Golding, Goulden) 24, 33, 36, 38, 41, 43, 46, 49, 51, 53, 56, 58, 59, 62
Gowers (Gore) 5, 6, 16, 19, 22, 24, 27, 29, 31, 33, *37, 40, 42, *44, 47, 50, 52, 55, 59, 60
Grarman (see Jarman &c.)
Gray (Grey) 8, 11, 21, 24, 26, 28, 30, 39, 41, 43, 46, 47, 48, 50, 51, 53, 54, 57, 59, 61, 62
Greeke 40
Green (Greene) 13, 15, 17, 20, 54, *60
Greenal (Greenall) 32, 33, 35, 38, 40, 42, 45, 50, 54, 55
Gregory (see Jregory)
Griffin 33, 40, 43, 45, 50
Griggs 41
Groten (Grooten) 40, 43, 45, 50

HACK 1, 2, 3, 4, 14, 17, 20, 21, 24, 25, 28, 30, 32, 34, 35, *36, *39, 41, 43, 46, 49, 51, 53, 56, 59, 62
Haggaman (Hagaman) 1, 2, 3

INDEX

Hall 3, 4, 5, 6, 10, 11, 13, 15, 16, 17, *20, 21, 24, 25, 28, 30, *32, 50
Haly (Halle, Hallie) 27, 30, 35, 39, 45, 50
Hamerin (Hamering, Hainering, Hammering) 7, 9, 10, 15, 17, 21, 23, *25, 28, 30, 31, 34, 37, 38, 41
Hamlin (Hamling) *3, 5, *7
Hammon (Hamon, Hammond, Hamond) 2, 3, 4, 5, 7, 8, 9, 10, 12, 13, 15, 17
Hancock (Hancok) 18, 19, 23, 25, 27, 28, 31, 33, 35, 37, 40, 42, 45, 47, 49, 55
Hanning 15, 19, 22, 23, 26, 27, 29, 31
Harde 19
Hare 45
Hargis (Harges, Hargos, Hargress, Harguis) 27, 30, 31, 33, 35, 38, 40, 43, 45, 48, 50, 52, 56, 57, 61
Harmon (Harman, Harmanson) 21, 23, 26, 30, 31, 33, 36, 38, 41, 44, 46, 51, 53, 56, 59, 62
Harrard (Harcard) 22, 23
Harris 12, 14, 16
Harrison (Harison) 3, 13, 14, 30, 32, 34, 36, 38, 39, 41, 42, 43, 44, *46, *48, *51, *53, *56, 58, 59, 61, 62
Hartley (Hartly) 47, 49, 54, 55
Harwood 25, 29, 31, 33, 35, 37, 40, 42, 44, 47, 49, 52, 59
Haselop (Hazelop, Hazelup) 36, 39, 41, 43, 46, 49, 51
Hastings (Hasting) 19, 22, 25, 27, 29, 31, 33, 37, 40, 42, 44, 47, 50, 52, 55, 57, 60
Hawley (Hawly, Hawlie) 32, 34, 47, 54
Hayes (Haies, Haze, Hase) 35, 37, 46, 47, 50, 55, 57
Hazard (Hasard) 50, 55, 58, 60
Heath 6, 36, 38, 46, 49, 51
Hedge (Hedges) 19, 24
Hendrick (Henrick) 6, 47
Hepworth 6, 8
Herricks 5
Hester 22
Hewes (Hues) 49, 52, 57, 60

Hewitt (Huitt, Huet, Huett, Huats, Huit, Hewet) 1, *2, *4, 6, 7, 9, 10, 12, 14, 16, 19, 21, 24, 26
Hickman (Hickmon, Hickmer) 11, 12, 18, 22, 26, 27, 29, 42, 48, 50, 54, *55, *57, 60, *61
Hicknet (Hignet) 1, 2
Higgs 6
Hill *1, 2, *3, *4, *5, *6, 7, *8, *9, *10, *12, *14, 15, *16, 17, *19, *21, *23, 24, 25, 26, 27, *28, *29, 32, 33, *34, 35, *36, *37, *39, 40, *41, *42, 43, *45, 46, 48, 50, 51, 56, 57, 58 *59, *61, 62
Hinderson 4
Hinman (Henimin) 7, 10, 12, 13, 16, 18, 19, 22, 23, 24, 27, *29, 32, 34, 37, 39, 41, 43, 45, 47, 49, 54, 57, *61
Hinton 41, 59
Hitchin (Hitching, Hittchin, Hitchins, Hichin, Hiching) 3, 5, 6, 7, 9, 10, 13, 15, 17, 19, 21, 23, 25, 28, 29, 31, 33, 35, 38, 40, 43, 45, 47, *48, 50, *52, *55, 58, *61
Hodgkins 1, *2
Hodson (Hodeson) 15, 40
Holden (Holding, Houldin) 1, 2, 3, 4, 6, 7, 9, 10, 12, 14, 20, 21, 26, 28, 30, 32, 34, 36, 38, 41, 48
Holland 8, 9, 10, 14, 16, 17, 19
Holliday 21, 25, 35, 38
Holliway 44
Hooke 46, 48, 51, 53, 58, 62
Hooton 40, 58
Hope 14, 21, 23, 25, 27, 29, 31, 33, 35, 38, 40, 42, 45, 47, 50, 54, 60
Hopkins *7
Hornsby (Hornbie) 23, 41
Houston 5
Houton (Huton, Hutton, Hutten, Heuton) 3, 42, 44, 48, 51, *53, *56, 60 62
Hoventon (Hoveington) 30, 32, 34, 36, 38, 41, 43, 46, 49, 53, 56, 59, 62
How 31, 33
Howard 38, 43
Howding 24
Hubanck (Ubanck) 31, 43, 47, 49
Huckson 21

69

INDEX

Hudder 37
Hudson (Hutson) 6 *16, 20, 24, 25,
  28, 32, 34, 35, 37, 42, 43, 44,
  45, 47, 48, 49, 50, 52, 54, 55,
  *57, 61
Huget 45
Hutchins 58
Hutchinson (Huchinson) *2, 4, 5, 6,
  7, 9, *10, 12, 14, 17, 20, 21, 24,
  26, 27, 28, 30, 32, 34, 36, 38,
  41, 43, 46, 48, 51, 53, *56, 59,
  62

IRONMONGER 43, 45, 50, 52, 55, 59, 61

JACOB 5, 7, *9, 13, 15, 17, 34, 41,
  43, 50, 56, 59
Jackson (Jacson) 1, 2, *3, 5, *7, 9,
  13, *15, 17, 20, 21, 24, 26, 28,
  30, *31, 33, 34, 36, *38, 40, 42,
  47, 49
Jacques (Jacquis, Lajaquith) 34, 57,
  61
James (Jeames) 6, 7, 9, 13, 15, 17,
  20, 42, 44, 46, 49
Jarman (Jarmon, Jerman, Grarman,
  German, Germane) 8, 12, 18, 19,
  22, 23, 25, 29, 32, 34, 36, 39,
  41, 43, 45, 47, 50, 52, 58, 61
Jarvis (Garvace) 46, 48, 57, 60
Jeffery 10
Jenifer 11, 13, 15, 18, 19, *22, *26,
  29, 31, 33, 35, 38, 40, 42, 45,
  47, *50, 54, 55, 57, 61
Jenkins (Jenkin, Jinkins, Ginkins) 1,
  *2, 4, 5, 6, *8, 10, 12, 13, 14,
  17, 18, 21, 24, 25, 27, 28, *30,
  32, 34, 36, 39, 41, 42, 43, 44,
  *45, 46, 47, 48, 50, 51, 52, 53,
  54, 55, 56, 58, 61
Jenkinson 57, 60
Jennings 10
Jester 42, 44, *49, 52, 55, 57, 60
Jillit (see Gillet &c.)
Jnions (see Onions &c.)
Johnson *1, *2, *3, *4, *5, *6, *7,
  *8, *9, *10, 11, 12, *13, *15,
  *16, *17, 18, *19, *20, *21, *23,
  *24, *25, *26, *27, *28, *29, *30,
  *31, 32, *33, 34, 35, *36, *37,
  *38, *39, *40, *41, *43, *45, 47,
  48, *49, 50, 51, *52, *54, *55,
  *57, *58, *60, *61, 62
Jolly 2, 4, 5
Jones 2, *3, 5, 6, *7, 9, *12, 14,
  16, 17, 18, 23, 24, 27, *28, *29,
  *30, 31, *32, 33, 34, 35, 36, *38,
  39, 40, *41, 43, *45, *46, *47,
  50, 51, *52, 53, *54, 56, 57, 58,
  *59, 60, 62
Jordan (Jordain) 1, 2, 3, 7, 15, 20,
  21, 24, 25, 30, 32, 34
Joyne (Joynes) 13, 17, 20, 21, 23,
  24, 28, 30, 31, 36, 41
Jregory 17
Justice 29, 32, 34, 36, 39, 40, 43,
  45, 47, 49, 52, 55, 57, 60

KEEBLE 6
Kellam (Kellum) 1, 2, 3, 4, 5, 6, 7,
  9, 10, *12, 13, *15, *16, 20, *21,
  *24, *26, 27, *28, 29, *30, 31,
  *32, *34, *36, *39, *41, *43, 44,
  *45, *46, 48, 49, *50, *53, *56,
  *59, *61
Kelly (Kelley) 1, 2, 3, 5, *7, 9, 11,
  13, 15, 17, 20
Kennet (Kennett, Kenet, Kennit) 8,
  11, 12, 18, 19, *22, 25, 27
Key 52, 55, 58, 60
King 1
Kirkman (Kerkman) 8, 9, 11, 12, 16,
  20, 51, 56, 59, 62
Knight 43, 45, 47, 50, 52, 55, 57, 60
Kude 52

LAJOQUITH (see Jacques)
Lambert 32, 33
Lambertson (Lamberson) 54, 55, 57, 61
Lamkin 11
Lane 40
Lang 59
Langford 45, 47, 50, 54, 57
Langsheare 47
Lawrence (Lawrance, Laurance,
  Larance) 1, *3, 4, *7, 9, 11, 13,
  17, 45
Laws (Law, Lawes) 17, 18, 19, 21, 23,
  25, 28, 30, 32, 34, 35, 39, 42,
  44, 46, 47, 51, 53, 56, 58, 62
Lay 61
Laylor (Laylar, Layler, Lailor,
  Laler) 5, 6, 7, 9, 10, 13, 15, 17,

INDEX

20, 21, 23, 25, 28, 30, 38, 41, 54, 59, 61
Leary 61
Leatherbury (Leatherberry, Letherbury) 1, 2, 3, 4, 5, 6, 8, 9, 10, *13, 15, 19, 21, 23, 25, 30, 32, 34, *36, *39, 42, *44, 45, 46, *48, *51, 53, 56, 58, 61
Lecat (LeCat, LeCatt) 4, 6, 7, 9, 10, 12, 14, 17, 20, 21, 24, 26, 28, 30, 32, 34, 36, 39, 41, 43, 46, 49, 51, 53, 56, *59, *62
Lee (Leegh, Leigh) 25, 28, 33, 37, 40, 42
Lenham 16
Lerkman 14
Lewis *1, 2, 3, 4, 5, 6, *8, 10, 12, 16, 17, *19, 21, 22, 23, 24, 25, 26, 27, 28, 29, *32, 33, *34, *36, *39, *41, 43, 44, 45, 48, 51, 52, 53, 54, 55, 56, 57, *58, *61, 62
Licence (Lijence, Lissons, Lysons) 34, 50, 52, 55, 57, 61
Lilliston (Lillyston, Lillingstone) 42, 44, 51, 61
Lingo 15, 25, 34, 36, 39, 41, 44, 45, 48, 51, 52, 59, 61
Liston *8, 10, 47
Litchfield (Lichfield, Leachfield, Leitchfeild) 27, 29, 32, 43, 45, 50, 54, 57, 61
Littlehouse 9, 14, 48, 51, 53, 58, 59, 62
Littleton 1, 2, 3, 4, 5, 6, 7, 9, *10, 12, *14, 16, 20, 21, *22, 23, 26, 27, *28, *41, *43, 46, 48, *51, 53, 54, 55, 56, 57, 58, *60
Lizium 41
Longo 1, 2, 3, 4, 6, 7, 13, 16, 20, 21, 24, 25, 28, 30, 32, 34, 36, 38, 41, 43, 46, 49, 51, 53, 56, 59, 62
Lory 51
Lowin (Lowing, Lowen) 8, 11, 12, 16, 18, 22, 23, 24, 26, 32
Lucas (Lucus, Lewcus) 26, 30, 31, 34, 36, 38, 40, 42, 45, 47, 49, 52, 55, 57, 60
Lurton (Lurtin, Lursen) 13, 15, 17, 20, 23, 26, 27, 29, 32, 33, 35, 38, 40, 43, *45, 48, 50, 52, 55, 58, 61

MACKARTY (Makarty) 12, 24 25
Mackemy (Mackemie, Mackenny) 44, 46, 48, 51, 53, 56
Mackerly 21
Mackhendrick (Mackhenry) 52, 55, 58, 60
Macklamme (Macktla my, Macglamen, Macklanne, Macklanen, Maclame, Mackelamny, Macklony, Maclonny, Macklany, Macklanie) 5, 8, 10, 12, 16, 17, 19, 22, 23, 25, 27, 29, 32, 34, 36, 39
Macknall 47
Macomb (Macome, Macom, Mecom, Mecome) 12, 15, 16, 19, 21, 24, 25, 28, 30, 34
Macra 1
Mackwilliam (Macwilliams, Maxwilliam) 5, 6, *8, 10, 12, 16, 18, 19, 22, 23, 29, 32, 57, 61
Madox (Maddox, Maddux, Madux, Maddex) 11, 13, 15, 17, *20
Major *1, 2, *3, 5, 6, 7, 9, 10, 13, 15, 16, 20, 21, *24, 28, 30, 32, 36, 38, 41, 43, 46, 49, 51, 56, 59, 62
Man 1
Mannington 35
Marrien 14
Marriner 8, 10, 23, 33, 35, 38, 40, 43, 45, 48, 50, 53
Marshall (Martiall) 2, 3, 5, 6, *7, 8, 9, 10, 11, 12, 13, 15, *17, 19, 20, 21, 22, 23, 24, 25, 26, *27, 29, 30, 31, 32, *33, 35, 36, *38, 40, 41, 43, 47, 50, *54, *55, 57, 58, 60
Martin (Martino) 8, 10, 16, 45, *49, 52, 57, 60
Marvill (Marvell, Marvel) 4, 5, 6, 7, 9, 11, 13, 18, 19, 50
Mason 8, 9, 10, 12, 14, 15, 18, 19, 22, 27, 30, 32, 34, 37, 39, 42, 44, 46, 51, 53, 54, 55, 56, 58, 59, *61
Massey (Massy, Marcy, Massee, Mercy) 3, 4, 5, 6, *8, 10, 13, 16, 19, *22, 26, 27, 29, 31, 33, 35, 37, 40, 42, 44, 47, 49, 52, *55, *58, 60
Mather 10
Mathews 33, 42, 55

INDEX

Matts 14, 17, 18, 21, 23, 26, 28, 30, 32, 36, 42
Meage 20
Meares (Meers, Meeres) 3, 4, 6, 7, 9, 10, 13, 15, 17, 18, 22, 23, 25, 27, 29, 31, 33, 35, *40, 43, 45, 49, 50, *52, 55, 59, *61
Medcalfe (Metcalfe) 15, 17, 18, 21, 23, 25, 27, 29, 31, 33, 35, 38, 40, 43
Mekittick 2
Mellony (Melony) 32, 48, 52, 55
Melson (Millson, Mellson) 16, 19, *22, 25, 26, 27, 28, 29, 31, 33, 37, 40, 58
Melton (Meltin) 20, 24, 30, 32, 34, 36, 38, 41, 43, 46, 49, 50, 52, 55, 58, 61
Merrell (Merrill) 38, 40, 45, 47
Michael (Mikeele, Mikeel, McKeel, Mackeel, Mickell, Mcall, Mecale, Macele) 1, 3, 4, 5, *6, *7, *8, *9, 10, 11, 12, 13, 14, 15, 16, *17, 18, 19, 20, 21, 22, 25, 27, 29, 31, *33, 35, 40, 43, *45, 48, 50, 53, 56, 61
Middleton (Midleton) 8, 10, *16, 18, 19, *22, 25, 26, 29, 32, *34, *36, 38, 39, *41, *43, 45, 46, 47, 48, 50, 51, 53, 54, 56, 57, 59, 61, 62
Milby (Millby) 1, 4, 20, 21, 24, 26, 28, 30, *32, 34, 36, 38, *41, *43, *46, *49, *51, *53, *56, *59, *62
Miles 12, 15, 18, 19, 22, 23, 26, 27, 29, 34, 35, 38, 40, 43, 45, 47, 49, 57, 61
Millard 2
Miller 1
Millichop (Milechop, Milechop) 12, 15, 18, 19, 21, 23, 25, 28, 30, 31, 33, 35, 37, 40, 42, 45, 47, 49, 52, 55, 57, 58, 60
Millington 27, 30
Mills (Milles) 24, *35, 43, *45, 47, 49, 52, 54, 55, 57, 60
Millyon 60
Milman (Milmon) 58, 60
Minshall 1, 2, 3
Miscall (Miskell, Misckell) 6, 8, 13, 19, *22, 25, 27, 29, 31, 33
Monford (Mountford, Mounford) 17, 18, 21
Monfreson 29
Monke (Monk, Munck) 39, 41, 43, 46, 49, 51, 53, 56, 59, 62
Moore (Moor, More) 1, 2, 3, 4, 5, *6, 8, *10, 13, 19, 20, 25, 29, 31, 33, 35, 37, 40, *42, *45, *47, *50, 52, 55, 58, 60
Moorecock 33
Morgan (Morgin, Morgen) *12, 18, 19, *22, 23, 24, 25, *26, *27, 29, 31, 33, *35, 37, 40, *42, 44, *45, 46, *47, *48, 49, 51, 52, 53, 55, 56, 57, 58, 59, *62
Morris (Morrish, Mores) 10, *12, *16, 18, *19, 22, 23, 24, 25, 27, 28, 29, 32, 33, 35, 38, 40, 42, 44, 45, 47, 49, 52, 55, 57, *60
NATES (Notes) 48, 50, 53
Natane 14
Natbolt 16
Needham (Needeme) 52, 60
Nelson (Nellson) 16, 18, 20, 21, 23, 25, 28, 30, 32, 34, 35, 36, 39, 41, 43, 44, *46, *48, *51, *53, 55, 56, 58, 60
Newcom (Nucomb) 19, 25
Newman (Numan) 26, 27, 29, 32, 34, 36, 40
Newton (Nuton) *1, 6, *8, 10, 12, 14, 17, 19, 23, 26, 27, *30, 32, 34, 36, 39, 40, 42, 44, 47, 49, 52, 55, 58, 60
Niblet (Niblett, Neblet) 4, 6, 9, 10, 12, 14, 17, 19, 21, 24, 25, 28, 30, 32, 34, 36, 38, 41, 43, 46, 48, 51, 53, 59, *62
Nicholson (Nickolson, Nickollson) *48, 51, 53, 56, *59, 61, 62
Nightingale 45
Nixson (Nixcon, Nickson) 13, 19, 22, 23, 25, 27, 29, 32, 34, 37, 39, 41, 42, 50, 54, 57, 60
Noble 60
Nock 9, 10, 13, 15, 17, 18, 21, 23, 25, 28, 29, 31, 33, 35, 38, 40, 43, 45, 48, 50, 52, 55, 58, 61
Norton 18, 49, 53, 55, 57, 60
Nubold 18, 19
Nussay 36

INDEX

OATES 17
Obin (Obben) 1, 2, 3, 5, *7, 9, 10
Ockohaid (Ockahone, Occahon) 6, 13, 16
Ocolnon (see Collony &c.)
Odobby 9
Ogleby 56, 58, 61
Ograhan (Ogragon, Ogreyhan, Ograyan) 1, *2, 4, 5, 6, 7, 9, 10, 12, 14, 20, 21, 24, 26, 27, 30, 32, 35, 36, 38, 41, 43, 46, 48, 51, 53, 56, 59, 62
Oheavens 44
Oliver (Ovila) 5, 12, 16, 17, 27
Onely (Only) 19, 25, 28, 30, 32, 34, 36, 55
Onions (Onion, Onyons, Jnions) 16, 18, 23, 25, 27, 29, 31, 33, 35, 38, 40, 43, 44, 47, 50, 54, 55, 57, 61
Onoughton (Onoughten, Onought, Onorton, Anaughten) 4, 8, 12, 16, 19, 22, 23, *26, 29
Oryly 43
Osborne (Osbourne, Osburne, Osburn) 4, 5, 6, 19, 22, 23, 25, 26, 27
Otters 18
Owen 10, *15, *17, 19, 21, 22, *23, *25, 28, 30, 31, 35, 37, 40, 42, 44, 49, 52, 55, 59, 60

PAGE 40, 43, 46, 47, 50, 52
Paine 40, 42, 44, 49, 52, 55
Painter 17
Palmer 28
Paramore (Paramoore, Parrimor, Parramor, Paramor, Parremore) 1, 2, *3, *4, *5, 6, *7, 9, 10, 11, 13, 15, 16, *17, *20, 21, 24, 25, 27, 30, 31, 33, 36, 38, 41, 50, 52
Paritson 23
Parkar (Perker) (*1, *2, 3, 4, *5, *6, *8, *9, *10, 12, *13, *14, 15, *17, *19, 21, *22, *23, *25, *26, *27, 28, *29, *30, *31, *32, *33, 34, *35, 36, *38, *39, *40, 41, 42, *43, *44, *45, 46, *47, *48, 49, 50, *51, *53, *54, 55, 56, *57, *58, *60, 61, *62
Parke 25, 28

Parks (Parkes) 13, 15, 17, 20, 21, 23, 24, 30, 34, 46, 47, 50, 54, 57, 60, 61
Parsons (Persons) 16, 17, 18, 19, 22
Partrige 10
Pash 60
Patrick 4, 5
Patterson (Paterson, Pattison) 47, 49, 52, 55, 58, 60
Peale (Peell) 13, 17
Pepper 3, 7
Permaine (Pairmame) 8, 13, 15
Perring 48, 51
Perret 18
Perry (Perrey) 10, 34, 40, 42, 44, 45, 47, 49, 52, 53, 55, 56, 58, 59, 60, 62
Pert 46
Peterson 44
Pettijohn (Pettejohn) 33, 38, 40, 43, 45, 48, 50
Phillby (Philby, Philbe, Filby) 19, 21, 23, 26, 28, 32, 36, 39
Phillips 32, 34, 36, 39, 42, 44, 46, 48, 51, 53, 56, 58, 60
Phiney (see Finney &c.)
Pike 6, *8
Pilcher (Pilsher) 32, 34, 38, 41, 43, 46, 49, 51, 53, 56, 59, 62
Pinfold 14
Pitman (Pittman) 7, 9, 10, 16, 20, 21
Pitts (Pitt) 2, 4, 5, 49, 53, 56, *57, 59, 61
Poaper 39
Pope 12, 14
Popelwell 40
Powell 9, 17, 20, 21, 32, 36, 39, 42, 44, 47, 50, 52
Powncy 57
Pratt *49, 51, 53, 56, 59, *62
Price 1, 2, 16, 40, 43, 45, 47, 49, 50, 52, *55, 60
Pritchard (Prichard, Pritchett, Prichet, Prichd., Pritcherd) 1, 4, 6, 9, 10, 13, 14, 17, 19, 21, 24, 26, 27, 30, 32, 34, 36, 39, 42, 44, *45, *48, *51, *53, *56, *58, 61, 62
Prittyman (Prittiman, Pritteman, Prettiman, Pretiman, Preteman) 1, 2, 3, 6, 7, 9, 11, 13, 15, 17, 18,

INDEX

19, 22, *23, *25, *27, 29, *31, 34, 37, 42, 47, 49, 52, 55, 57, 60
Prophet 26, 27, 31
Prossit 29
Pywell (Piwell) 9, 10, 12, 14, 17, 21, 24, 26, 28, 29, 32, 34, 36, 39, 58, 62

QUILLIAN 2
Quinton 8, 19, *24, 27, 30, 32, 34, 36

RAHAN 19
Ramsy (Ramsee, Ramsie, Ramse) 29, 31, 33, 35, 37, 40
Ramy 1
Rapishare (Rapishaw, Rappishaw) 5, 6, 9
Ratclife (Ratclift, Ratliff, Rackliff, Rackleff, Radeliff) 1, 2, 3, 4, 5, 6, *8, 11, 12, 15, 18, 19, 22, 23, 25, 27, 29, 31, 33, 35, 37, 40, 42, 44, 47, 49, 54, 55, 58
Rawlins 41, 44, 51, 53, 56, 58
Reade (Read) 12, 14, 16, 17, 20, *21, *24, 25, 26, 27, 28, *30, *32, 33, 34, *36, *38, 40, 42, 44, 46, *48, *51, *53, 55, 56, *59, *60, 62
Rennalls 55
Renny (Reney, Renney, Ranny) 2, 3, 4, 5, 6, *8, 12, 13, 16, 18, 19, 22
Revell (Revill, Revel) 1, 2, 3, 4, 5, 6, 7, 9, 10, 13, *15, 17, 18, 21, 24, 25, 27, 30, 32, 34, 35, 38, 42, 43, 45, 48, 50, 53, 56, 58, 61
Rew-Rou (see Arew &c.)
Rich 55
Richards (Ricords, Rickords, Ricketts) *1, 3, 4, 5, *6, *7, *9, *10, 25, 28, 34, *43, *46, 47, 48, 49, *51, *53, 55, *56, 57, *59, 61, *62
Richardson (Richison) 2, 3, *4, 6, 7, 32, 39, 42, 44, 46, 51, 53, 56, 58, 62
Richinson (Richenson) 1, 36
Ridin 49
Right (see Wright)
Rigon (Regon, Regan) 10, 12, 15, 17, 19

Riley (Rila, Rilack, Rilie, Ryly, Ryley, Ryle, Reyly, Ryla) 3, 6, *8, 10, 12, 16, 19, 23, 26, 27, 29, 32, 34, 36, 41, 45, 48, 49, 50, 54, 55, 57, 61
Riping (Ripping) 57, 60
Roberts (Robts.) 1, 2, 3, 4, 5, *7, *9, 10, 11, 13, 17, 19, 20, 21, 23, 25, 28, 30, *33, 34, 36, 38, 41, 44, 46, 48, 53, 59, 61, *62
Robins 9, 10, 13, *15, 16, 20, 21, 24, 26, 28, 30, 31, 32, 33, 36, 38, 41, 43, 47, 49, 51, 52, 55, *58, *60
Robinson 5, 6, 8, 9, 11, 12, *15, 18, 26, 34, 39, 42, *44, 45, *46, *48, 50, *51, 52, *53, 55, 58, 60, 61
Rodgers (Rogers) 18, 19, 23, 36, 39, 41, 42, 43, 44, 45, *46, 47, 48, *49, *50, *51, *52, 53, 54, 55, *56, 58, *59, 60, 61, *62
Rodolphus 1, 2
Row (Roe) 15, 20, 21, 23
Rowles (Roles, Rolles, Roules) *8, 10, 12, 14, 16, 20, 21, 24, 25, 28, 30, 32, 34, 36, 38, 41, 43, 46, 49, 51, 53, 56, 59, 62
Royle 22
Russell 3, 12, 24, 28, 34, 36, 38
Rust 12, 14, 16, 21, 32, 35
Ryding (Riding, Rideing) 13, 15, 16, 17, *20, 62

SACKER (Sacaker) 4, 5, 6, *8, 11, 35, 40
Sadbrook 10
Sadbury (Sadberry, Sadbery) 17, 18, 21, 24, 25, 28, 29, 30, 31, 49, 52
Sadler 14
Sample 35, 40, 50
Samson 41
Sanders 7, 40, 47, 50, 54, 57, 61
Sanford (Sandford) 23, 24, 26, 28, 29, 31, 37, 38, 40, 42, 46, 47, 49, 52, 55, 59, 60
Sankhills 45
Savage (Savadge, Savedge, Savidge) *3, *4, *6, *8, 9, 10, 12, *13, 14, 15, *16, *17, 18, 19, *20, *21, 23, *24, *25, *28, 30, *32, *34, 36, *38, *41, 43, 44, *46, *48, *51, *53, *56, *59, *62

74

INDEX

Scanel (Scannell, Scanell, Scamell)
9, 11, 13, 15, 17, *20, 25, 32,
34, 36
Scarburgh *2, 3, 4, 5, *6, 7, 9, 10,
*11, 12, 13, *14, *15, 16, 17, 18,
*19, 20, *21, 23, 24, 25, *26,
*28, *29, 30, *32, *34, *36, 38,
39, *41, 42, 43, *44, *46, *48,
51, *53, *56, 58, 59, 61, *62
Scott (Scot, Stott) 1, 2, 3, 4, 5, 6,
7, 9, 11, 13, 15, *17, 20, 22, 24,
*28, 30, 32, 34, 36, 39, 41, 44,
46, 49, 53, 55, 56, 57, 60
Scudamore 26
Seaward 62
Selby (Selve, Sellvey, Selbye, Selvy)
1, *2, *3, *4, 5, 6, 7, 9, 10, 12,
14, 16, 20, 21, 24, 26, 28
Sellings 40
Selman (Sellman) 10, 14, 16, 20, 24,
25, 28, 30, 32, 41, 43, 46, 48,
51, 53, 56, 59, 62
Sempler 38
Senlet 60
Sentless 49
Serjeant (Serjent, Serjant) 12, 15,
16, 20, 23, 26, 28, 30, 32, 34,
36, 38, 41
Sevorne 3
Sharpe 60
Sharplys 34
Sheale 13, 17, 20
Shelleto 6
Shepheard (Shephard, Sheppard,
Sheperd, Shepherd, Shepard) 3, 5,
9, 10, 13, 15, 17, 20, 21, 24, 26,
*28, 30, 31, 34, 35, 36, 38, 41,
42, 47, 49, *52, 54, 57, *60, 62
Sherwood *2, 4
Ship (Shipp) 10, 12, 14, 16, 20, 21
Shore (Shores, Shere) 41, 43, 55
Showell (Shewell) 3, 4, 6, 9, 10
Sikes 6, 8, 11
Sill 15, 23, 26, 32, 34, 36, 39, 42,
44, 46, 49, 51, 53, 56, 59, 62
Silverthorne 1, 2, 3, 4, 5, 6, 8, 9,
10, 12, 14, 17, 18, 21, 23, 26,
27, 29, 32, 34, 36, 38, 40, 47,
49, 53, 55, 58, 61
Simcock (Simcok) 27, 32, 34, 36, 38,
41, 43, 46, 49, 51, 56, 58, 61
Simons (Symons) 28, 60
Simpson (Simson) 35, 38, 41, 43, 45,
47, 49, 53, 57, 61
Skiner 6
Slaterfeild 44
Smally (Smalley, Smalle, Small) 4, 5,
*6, 7, *8, 9, *10, 12, 14, *16,
18, *21, *22, 24, *25, 26, 28, 30,
32, 34, 36, 38, 41, 43, 54, 57
Smalpeece (Smalpec) 12, 19
Smith *1, *2, *3, *4, *5, *6, *7, *8,
*9, *10, *11, 12, *13, 14, *15,
16, *17, *18, 19, *20, *21, *22,
*23, *24, 25, 26, *27, 28, *29,
*30, *31, *32, *33, *34, 35, *36,
37, *38, *40, 41, 44, 45, 46, 47,
48, 49, 50, 51, *52, *53, *55,
*56, *57, *58, 59, 60, *61, 62
Smothers (Smuthers) 34, 37, 42, 47
Snelon 56
Snow 15
Souses 41
Southern 9, 23
Sparkes 32, 36, 39, 41, 43
Spencer 13, 16
Spires (Spiars) 30, 32, 34, 36, 39,
41, 43, 46, 49, 50, 52
Stakes 36, 40, 43, 45, 48, 50, 52,
56, 58, 61
Staneworth 58
Stanley (Stanly, Stannly, Standly)
*12, 15, 18, 19, *22, 24, 45
Stanton (Stainton) 30, 37, 39, 41,
44, 46, 48, 51, 53, 56, 58
Stevens (Steavens) 1, 16, 20
Stewart (Steward, Stuart) 36, 39, 41,
43, 46, 48, 50, 53, 56, 59, 62
Stills 12
Stockley (Stockly, Stoackly,
Stockely, Stokely, Stokly,
Stokeley) 8, 11, *12, 15, *17, *18,
*19, *22, *23, *24, *25, 26, *27,
*29, *31, *33, *35, *37, *40, *42,
*44, *47, *49, *52, *55, 57, *58,
*60
Stopp (Stop, Stope) 19, 21, 24, 26,
28, 29, 32, 34, 36, 39, 41, 44,
46, 48, 51, 56, 62
Stratton (Straton, Stretton) 12, 14,
15, 19, 22, 23, 24, 27, 29, 31,
33, 35, 39, 40, 44, 47, 49, 52
Stringer 18, 23, 26, 28
Stripe (Stripes) 52, 54, 55, 57, 60

INDEX

Studson (Stutson) 1, 2,
Sturgis (Sturges, Storges) 2, 6, 8, 11, *12, 15, 18, 19, 22, 23, 26, 27, 29, 31, 33, 35, 41, 42, 43, 45, *47, 50, *54, 57, 60
Sullevan (Selevant, Sellevan, Shellowan, Swilliam, Selivant, Sullivent, Sullivan, Sellivant, Sulivant) 1, 3, *4, *6, *7, *9, 10, 11, 13, *15, 16, 17, 19, 20, 21, *24, 25, 26, 28, 30, 32, 34, 36, 39, 41, 43, 46, 48, 51
Supple (Sipple) 17, 19, 21, 24, 25, 42, 47, 49, 52, 54, 58, 60
Sutars (Suiters) 54, 58
Symmont 19

TALSBY 37
Tankred (Tankark) 15, 23, 25, 27
Tanner 26, 34, 36, 39, 46
Tarr 19, 22, 23, 35
Tatham (Tathan, Tathum, Tathem) 32, 33, 48, 50, 54, 55, 57, 60
Taylor *1, *2, *3, *4, *5, *6, 7, *8, *9, *10, 11, *12, *13, *14, *15, *16, *17, *18, *19, *20, *21, *22, *23, *24, *25, *26, *27, *28, *29, 30, *31, 32, *33, *34, 35, *36, *37, *38, 39, *40, *41, *42, *43, *44, *45, *46, *47, *48, *49, *50, *51, *52, *53, *54, *55, *56, 57, *58, *59, *60, *61, *62
Teackle (Teakle, Teagle) 12, 14, 16, 20, 21, 24, 26, 28, 30, 32, 34, 36, 38, 41, 43, 45, 46, 49, 51, 56, 59, 62
Teage (Tege) 2, 9, *13, 15, 28
Terry (Terrey) 18, 29, 31, 33, 43
Therrit 29
Thomas 12, 13, *14, 16, 19, 21, 25, 28, 31, 33, 35, 38, 39, 40, 41, 60
Thompson (Tompson, Thomson, Tomson) 3, 4, 5, *7, 8, 9, *11, 12, 15, 17, 18, 19, 20, *22, 23, *25, 26, *27, 29, 32, 36, 39, *41, 42, 44, 45, 46, 47, 49, 50, 51, 53, 54, 55, 56, 58, 59, 60, 62
Thorne 23, *43, 45, 48, 50, 54, 57, 61
Thornton (Thorton, Thoroton, Thorneton) 19, 23, 25, 26, 28, 29, 30, 31, 32, 33, 34, 35, 36, 37, 39, 41, 42, *44, 46, 47, 48, 49, 51, 52, 55, 57, 60
Thornbury (Thorneberry) 36, 39, 44, 58, 61
Thureton 53
Tike 4
Tilney (Tillny, Tinly, Tinley, Tylney, Tildgly) 1, 2, 3, 4, 5, *7, 9, 11, 13, 15, 17, 20, 37, 45, 48, 50, 53, 56, 59, 61
Tinsby 5
Tire 53
Tiron 14
Tissaker (Tisseker, Tisaker, Tusszacar, Tisacar, Tizacar, Tisiker, Tusicur) 30, 32, 34, 36, 39, 42, 44, 46, 48, 51, 53, 56, 58, 61
Toft 4, 5, *8, 23
Toldersbee 49
Tomlinson 8
Toulderbury 47
Tounsend (Tounson, Tounsen, Touning) 13, 18, 19, 22, 23, 25, *27, 29, 32, 34, *35, 37, 40, *42, 45, 46, *49, 54, 52, 55, 58, 60
Towles (Toules) 26, 27, 29, 31, 33, 35, 37, 40, 42, 44, 47, 49, 52, 54, 59, 60
Towser (Tozer) 53, 56, 58
Traffick 17
Trafford 18, 23
Travally 6, 15, 21, 23
Trotman 2
Trueman (Truman, Trewman) *7, 9, 11, 13, 15, 17, 20
Truitt (Truett, Truet, Trewit, Trewett) 1, 2, 3, 4, 5, 6, *8, *10, *12, *16, *18, 19, 22, 25, 27, *29 *32, 34, 36, 37, *39, 41, 42, *45, 47, 50, 58, 61
Trught 27
Tryar 16
Tubbin (Tubbins) 5, 6, 7, 9, 11, 13, 17, 20
Tuck 17
Tucker 54
Tull 49
Tunnell (Tunell, Tunnill, Tunnel) 1, 2, 3, *4, 6, 8, 9, 30, 31, 33, 35, 37, 40, 42, 44, 47, 50, 52, 55, 57, 60

INDEX

Turlington 53, 56
Turnon (Ternal, Ternan, Turnell, Ternall, Ternon, Ternion) *5, 6, *8, 10, 12, 17, 19, 22, 23, 26, 27, 29, 32, 34, *36, 39, 41, 43, 45, 47, 50, 54, 57
Turnor (Turner) 1, 2, *3, 24, 25
Tutchberry 27, 30
Twyford (Twiford) 33, 35, 38, 40, 43, 48, 50, 52, 55, 58, 61
Tyler (Tiler, Tyer) 9, 20, 21, 24, 26, 28, 30
Tyson (Tison) 59, 62

UBANCK (see Hubanck)
Uell (see Ewell)
Upshur (Upshor, Upshot, Upshott) 1, 4, 7, 10, 13, 22, 23, 24, 28, 29, 31, 33, 35, 38, 40, 43, 45, 48, 50, 52, 55, 58, 61

VAN NITSIN (Vannitsin, Van Nelson, Vanelson, Vannetson, Vanilson, Van Nitzon, Venetson, Van Etsan, Vannelson, Van Natson) 2, 4, 5, *7, 9, 11, 12, 15, 18, 19, 22, 23, 26, 27, 29, 35, 37, 40, 42, 45, 49, 52, 55, 60
Vaughan (Vahun, Vahan) 5, 6, *8, 11, 12, 15, 18, 22, 23, 25, 29
Verhoofe 10, 13

WAGGAMAN (Wagaman) 5, 6, 7, 10, 12, 17, 20, 21, 24, 25, 28, 40, 42, 44, 47, 49, 52, 55, 58, 61
Wagrah 50
Wainhouse 34, 36, 38, 41, 44, 46, 48, 51, 53, 56, 59, 62
Waite (Waight, Weight) *37, 40, *42, 49, 52, 58
Waler 1
Waley (Wayle, Wale, Walle) 12, 29, 34, 38, 41, 42, 43, 46, 48, 53, 56, 59, 62
Walford 7
Walker (Waker) 5, 6, *8, 9, 10, 11, 12, 13, *15, 17, 18, 19, 21, 22, *23, 24, 26, 27, 29, *31, 32, *33, 34, *35, 37, *38, *40, 41, 42, *43, *45, 46, 47, *48, 49, *50, 51, *52, 53, 55, *56, 58, *59, 60, *61, 62

Wallis 19
Wallop 2, 3, 4, 5, 6, 8, 9, 11, 12, 15, 18, *19, *22, 24, 27, *28, *33, *35, 37, *40, *42, *44, 47, 49, 50, *52, 55, 60
Wally 1
Walthom (Walthum, Waltom) 1, 2, 3, 4, 5, 6, 7, 9, 10, 12, 19, 21, 24, 25, 28, 30, 32, 34, 36, 39, 41, *43, 46, *49, *51, 53, *56, 59, *62
Walton 7, 11
Warder 37
Wardle (Wardell) 42, 48
Waring 34
Warren (Warrin) 18, 41
Warrington 17, 21, 24, 26, 28, 30, 32, *34, 36, 39, 44, 46, 48, 51, 53, 56, 58, 62
Washbourne 21, 24, 25, 28, 30, 32, 34, 36, 38, 41, 43, 46, 48, 51, 53, 56, 59, 62
Waters 53, 57
Wathen (Wathan) 27, 30
Watkin (Watkins, Wadkins) 34, 56, 58
Watkinson 5, 26, 28, 30, 32, 34, 36, 39, 41
Watson (Wattson) 1, 2, 3, 4, 5, 7, 9, 10, *12, 13, *17, *19, 20, *21, 23, *24, *25, 26, 27, 28, 29, *30, 31, *33, *36, *38, *41, 43, *44, *46, *48, *51, 52, *53, *56, 57, *59, *62
Watts 1, *2, *3, *4, *5, *6, *8, 10, 11, 13, 14, 15, 17, 18, *19, 21, *22, 24, *26, *27, *29, 31, 32, 33, 35, 40, 42, 44, 47, *49, 51, 52, *55, 58, 59, 60
Webb 15, 18, 19, 26, 27, 30, 32, 34, 36, 39, 43, 46, 51, 53, 56, 58, 60
Webster 16
Weines 20
Welburn (Welborne, Welburne) *15, *22, 24, 28, *31, *33, *37, 40, 42, 46, *47, 50, 51, 57, 60
Welch (Weelch) 17, 20, 21, 35, 36, 40, 45, 48, 55, 57, 61
Welton 37
West 1, 3, 4, 8, 9, 11, 12, 13, 14, 15, 16, *18, *19, 21, 22, 23, 24, 25, *26, *27, 28, 29, 30, 31, *32, *34, 35, 37, 38, *39, 40, *42,

INDEX

*44, *45, *47, 48, *49, 50, *51, 52, *53, 55, *56, 57, *58, 59, *60, *61, 62
Wharton (Whorton) 8, 12, 16, 19, 22, 23, 25, 27, 29, 32, 34, 35, 37, 40, 42, 45, 46, 48, 50, 54, 55, 57, 58, 60
Wheatcraft 36
Wheatly 2, 56
Wheatmost 13
Wheeler 16, 18, 25, 27, 29, 31, 33, *35, 37, 38, *40, 43, 44, 45, *47, *49, 54, 57, 61
Wheelton 42, 44, 47, 49, 52, 55, 57, 61
White *1, *2, *3, *4, *5, *6, *7, 8, *9, *10, 12, *13, *14, 15, *16, *17, 18, 19, *20, *22, *23, 24, *25, 26, 27, *28, 29, *30, 32, 34, 36, 38, 41, 43, 46, 49, 51, 53, *56, 59, *62
Whitehead 36
Whittington 33, 37, 38, 40
Whittman 15, 16
Wilkinson 31, 40, 48
Will 36
Willet (Willett) 12, 24, 29, 41, 43, 45, 47, 50, 54, 57, 61
Williams 1, 2, 3, 4, 5, 9, 10, *11, *13, *15, 16, 17, 18, 19, *20, *21, *23, *24, 25, 27, 28, *29, 30, *31, 33, 35, 36, 38, 40, 45, 46, 51, 53, 56, 59
Williamson 2, 4, 5, 6, 8, 10
Willis (Willers) 3, 4, 7, 9,' 10, 11, 13, 15, 17, 18, 21, 23, 25, *28, 29, 31, 33, 35, 38, 43, *45, *48, *50, 52, *55, *58, *61
Willisome 3
Willowby (Willoughbye) 7, 9
Wilson (Willson) 2, 3, 6, 7, 9, 10, 15, 16, 17, 18, 21, 24, 25, 29, 30, 32, 34, 35, 36, 38, *40, 41, 43, 46, 48, 50, 52, 55, 57, 58, 61
Wimbrow (Wimburrow, Winburrow) 38, 42, 47, 54, 58
Wingood 4, 5
Wise *1, 2, 3, 4, 5, 6 *8, *10, 12, 13, *14, 17, 18, 19, 24, 25, 27, *30, 32, *34, *36, *39, 42, *46, *48, *51, *53, 56, *58, *61, 62
Withum 15

Wood 20, 30, 32, 45, 47, 49, *54
Woodland 43, 45, 47, 50, 54, 55, 57, 61
Wooslee (Woosle) 33, 35
Wouldhave (Woodhave) 16, 20, 21, 28, 31
Wreathwell 25
Wright (Whright, Right) 6, 7, 9, 17, 18, 25, 29, 31, 33, 35, 37, 40, 42, 43, 44, *49, 52, 54, 55, 57, 60
Wyat (Wyatt) 24, 27, 31, 33, 47, 55, 60

YEO (Yeow) 1, *2, 4, 5, 6, 7, 9, 10, 11, 14, 17, *20, 21, 43, 50, 54, 61
Yewell (see Ewell)
Yorke 14, 17, 24
Young 19, 49, 54, *57

www.ingramcontent.com/pod-product-compliance
Lightning Source LLC
Chambersburg PA
CBHW051701090426
42736CB00013B/2482